WAKE UP CALL FOR INDIAN REPUBLIC

WAKE UP CALL FOR INDIAN REPUBLIC

Justice V.R. Krishana Iyer

GYAN

Wake up Call for Indian Republic

Rs. 540

ISBN: 978-81-212-1045-4

Published in 2010 in India by
Gyan Publishing House,
23 Main, Ansari Road, Darya Ganj,
New Delhi-110002
Phones : 23282060, 23261060
Fax : 011-23285914
E-mail: books@gyanbooks.com
Website: www.gyanbooks.com

Lasser Type Setting by: Quick Media, Delhi
Printed at : Gian Ridhi Offset Printers, Delhi

Contents

Preface

I love reading books especially scholarly ones although that class of books is becoming rarer, and rarer because of the invasion of superficial literature. Not Babylon nor Greece nor Rome nor Egypt nor the most ancient manifestation of wisdom of homosapiens. It was Max Muller who researched and discovered that the source of vedic vintage was the most ancient and sublime of the earliest wisdom of humanity in the cultural history of the globe. It is fair to quote Max Muller on vedic literature at this point:

If we were to look over the whole world to find out the country most richly endowed with all the wealth, power, and beauty that nature can bestow - in some parts a very paradise on earth - I should point to India. If I were asked under what sky the human mind has most fully developed some of its choicest gifts, has most deeply pondered over the greatest problems of life, and has found solutions of some of them which well deserve the attention even of those who have studied Plato and Kant - I should point to India. And if I were to ask myself from what literature we here in Europe, we who have been nurtured almost exclusively on the thoughts of Greeks and Romans, and of one Semitic race, the Jewish, may draw the corrective which is most wanted in order to make our inner life more perfect, more comprehensive, more universal, in fact more truly human a life, not for this life only, but a transfigured and eternal life - again I should point to India.

The great culture of Greece was perhaps more decidedly the finest of the West but Rome with its might and material splendour rose to occupy the highest cultural altitude and pushed Greeks into the rear. When the cultural history of a western world comes to be written, the world's seven wonders will be Babylon, the capital of the Babylonian empire. Alexander the great was the supreme commander of the Greeks and in his imperial march, conquest after conquest came to the frontiers of India but was halted there. Then came the Roman Empire Ceaser after Ceaser and the top of the world and in the modern times industrial empires grew, the most powerful of which was the British Empire while French, Portuguese and Dutch failed to occupy India. The British made India part of the British Empire. But when objective study of humanity's cultural spiral comes to be recorded, there is none to equal the ancient glory or the cultural magnificence of the Buddha and Asoka. On Buddha the eloquent Vivekananda wrote:

Let me tell you a few words about one man who actually carried this teaching of Karma-Yogi into practice. That man is Buddha. He is the one man who ever carried this into perfect practice. All the prophets in the world, except Buddha, had external motives to move them to unselfish action. The prophets of the world, with this single exception, may be divided into two sets, one set holding that they are incarnations of God come down to earth, and the other holding that they are only the messengers from God; and both draw their impetus for working from outside, however highly spiritual maybe the language they use. But Buddha is the only prophet who said, "I do not care to know your various theories about God. What is the use of discussing all the subtle doctrines about the soul? Do good and be good. And this will take you to freedom and to whatever truth there is." He was, in the conduct of his life, absolutely without personal motives; and what man worked more than he? Show me in history one character who has soared so high above all. The whole human race has produced but one such character, such high philosophy, such wide sympathy, yet had the deepest sympathy for the lowest animals, and never put forth any claims for himself. He is the ideal Karma-Yogi, acting entirely without motive, and the history of humanity shows him to have been the greatest man ever born; beyond compare the greatest combination of heart and brain that ever existed, the greatest soul power that has ever been manifested. He is the first great reformer the world has seen. He was the first who dared to say, "Believe not because some old manuscripts are produced, believe not because it is your national belief, because you have been made to believe it from your childhood; but reason it all out, and after you have analysed it, then, if you find that it will do good to one and all, believe it, live up to it, and help others to live up to it." He works best who works without any motive, neither for money, nor for fame, nor for anything else; and when a man can do that, he will be a Buddha, and out of him will come the power to work in such a manner as will transform the world. This man represents the very highest ideal of Karma-Yogi.

In this procession of cultures and empires, India stands out towering the rest as Everest and Himalayas but now everyone submits as its valleys. This cultural depression and moral collapse is what India and the world is passing through.

Our generation with its little men have to be adventurous pioneers winning back the vedic glory once again in a transformation of spiritual and material reincarnation. About the great Asoka who abandoned war after victory, H.G. Wells wrote in his Outline of World History:

> *For eight-and-twenty years Asoka worked sanely for the real needs of men. Amidst the tens of thousands of names of monarchs that crowd the columns of history, their majestics and graciousnesses and serenities and royal highnesses and the like, the name of Asoka shines, and shines almost alone, a star. From the Volga to Japan, his name is still honoured. China, Tibet, and even India, though it has left his doctrine, preserve the tradition of his greatness. More living men cherish the memory today than ever heard the names of Constantine or Charlemagne.*

In this long march of rehabilitation, the discovery of our past milestone after milestone, is a patriotic roaming. It is in this context that I preserve the marvel of the vedic odyssey in every field of knowledge. We have a marvellous past in the philosophical pragmatic and spiritual ascent. Dr. C.K. Ramachandran has traveled deep in the oceanic floor of our ancient culture. The Upanishads are the philosophic pinnacle and the book "Medicine in Atharvaveda" will hold a high place in the world literature. The therapeutic ancient past of the East and the West including science of human health has a holistic unity which blossomed in the Atharvaveda. Read on the profound pages of the sacred book and you will realize who you are. The first task of patriotic research is to know oneself and continue to ask as our vedic ancients did *who am I?*

We have a timeless past, and countless accumulation of wisdom. The finest essence or the vedic conscience is crystalised in the numerous Upanishads of which the first ten were the subject of luminous commentaries of Adi Sankara. Vivekananda was inspired by this glorious ecstasy of erudition of Adi Sankara. Even Mahatma Gandhi on his impregnable commitment for truth and non-violence had his illuminating fire from the Vedas which began the verses with the first verse in the Rig Veda:

aa no bhadraah kratavo yantu vishvatah

Let noble thoughts come to us from every side— Rigveda, 1-89-I

How grand is this open universe of wisdom and the thought.

The soul of the Upansihads were not merely spiritual but material too because in Vivekananda's words:

We talk foolishly against material civilization. The grapes are sour...Material civilization, nay even luxury, is necessary to create work for the poor. Bread; I do not believe in a God, who cannot give me bread here, giving me eternal bliss in heaven. Pooh; India is to be raised, the poor are to be fed, education is to be spread, and the evil of priestcraft is to be removed...more bread, more opportunity for everybody...

The vedic ideology was not confined to moral and mental, not even psychic levels of supra-mental Brahminical intellectual ascent but Bharat's human health and evolutionary spiral for the elevation of caste-free global humanity since without material values the foundational basics of any nation's for the higher cultural development. Thus, it is in a holistic approach to cosmic Existence that our ancient Savants did their experiments with truth in all its panoramic angles and facets of public health and pharmaceuticals, cleanliness and sanitation in civic life, mental, moral, physical and intellectual, which were covered by the explanation by our saints, sages, philosophers and thinkers. Natural Medicine Systems and plural intellectual pursuits promotive of yogic community welfare, dealt within the Atharvaveda and sprinkled in other Vedas too, only antiquarian scholars, incisively interested in the profound and progressive depths of public health, could master these contributions of India through Ayurveda and other systems without artificial... animal meat. Now this Vedic wealth of the world is an integral part of universal life science through the WHO and other branches of oriental sciences. In India, our researchers conditioned by the materialist West, have slept over eastern light, which if revealed, would awaken the North and the West to the rare facets of the whole human health truth in its infinite dimensions. But truth unfolds through deep studies and informed research of these rare superficial days. One such scholar proficient in the discovery of our wisdom, our heritage derived from our ancestors is, Dr. C.K. Ramachandran rarest of the rare at the peak of pharmacopoeia, allopathic and ayurvedic, out of determination to gain learning from wherever it comes, not to make money but to unfold the glory of compassion and humanism towards all living creatures which is a patriotic duty under Article 53A of our Constitution. Dear Dr. Ramachandran, I salute you for this paradigmatic phenomenon. You are as a gift to mankind. Dr. Ramachandran has realized the deeper sources of divine life and its manifestation in supra moral and mental dimensions of dharma, which is a composite conception of vedic cult, not the monopolistic possession of the Hindus, nor of Bharat but is the wealth of the cosmos. It is not confined to the earth alone but of our solar planets and other stars. You need Sanskritic learning to get a glimpse of this multiverse of knowledge. Whitman, Emerson and Herbert Spencer, the German philosopher have disclosed in their inspirational writings:

I believe a leaf of grass is no less than the journey-work of the stars. And the pismire is equally perfect, and a grain of sand, and the egg of the wren,

And the tree toad is a chef-d' oeuvre for the highest,

And the running blackberry would adorn the parlors of heaven. *(Walt Whitman)*

Now Emerson

If the red slayer think he slays,

Or if the slain think he is slain,

They know not well the subtle ways

I keep, and pass, and turn again. (Brahman)

No one can be perfectly free till all are free; no one can be perfectly moral till all are moral; no one can be perfectly happy till all are happy. ***(Herbert Spencer)***

Now Witman

In the faces of men and women I see God, and in my own face in the glass,

I find letters from God dropt in the street, and every one is sign'd by God's name,

And I leave them where they are, for I know that wheresoe'er I go,

Others will punctually come for ever and ever.

Medicines in Atharvaveda is not, for me a store of Sanskrit verses but a movement, a rediscovery of ourselves, an encyclopaedic grandeur, dug up from our Vedic dynamic past to peep into the future to build a New World Order. It's a flame of hope that lights up the path of rediscovering ourselves through the infinite mirror of Vedas, of fertilising our collective future. Let me quote myself in conclusion:

The hallowed land of Bharat produced the Upanishads for the benefit of generations of humankind on earth and other planets wherever life may flourish. Humbler mortals like me may only gain a moment's glimpse and be astonished but a Rabindranath may sing, a Radhakrishnan may expound, an Aurobindo may experience, a Ramana or Sai Baba, a Nityananda or J. Krishnamurti may realize. Likewise, other saints and prophets in other

> *climes and countries may have had Upanishadic impulses, regardless of religion and sect. Truth is the same though it may have various versions and view-points. The greatest exponent of these songs Celestial or Upanishadic verses is Shankara whose brief mortal spell blessed mankind with boundless wisdom in its finest blossom, now in terse prose, now in superb poetry, now in bursts of devotional song, now in superb poetry, now in bursts of devotional song, now in harsh admonition to blind materialists and bigoted ritualists. Jèwels here, jewels there, jewels everywhere - such is the treasury of thought Sankara has left as legacy. We are heirs, but the heirs must become worthy of the heritage and the acharya. Vachaspati, spending a lifetime to learn, has played the mediator between the people who yearn - may their tribe increase!—and that matchless genius whose commentaries on the foremost ten Upanishads form the subject matter of this work coming out in many volumes (From the 'Foreword' to the Book Upanishads in Sankara's Own Words)*

Max Muller regarded Rig Veda 'the first word spoken by the Aryan man'. These Aryans envisioned Truth without inhibitions and asked deeper questions. Evolving from this vigorous investigation came the Upanishadic monism. Says Nehru:

> *"The Upanishads are instinct with a spirit of inquiry, of mental adventure, of a passion for finding out the truth about things. The search for this truth is, of course, not by the objective methods of modern science, yet there is an element of the scientific method in the approach. No dogma is allowed to come in the way." (The Discovery of India*-by Jawaharlal Nehru—p. 89)

My reverence for Dr. C.K. Ramachandran persuades me to quote another equally scholarly divine savant to whose Upanishadic work I wrote below which applies with greater relevance to Dr. C.K. Ramachandran:

The world of knowledge, of atman within and its universal projections without, remains to be discovered. Man must, in the spirit of abhay, dare to overcome inhibitions against enquiry and reach out to the stars which shine forth to tell us the truth. Jnana Marga is the key.

"It is said that desire for knowledge lost us the Eden of the past; but whether that is true or not, it will certainly give us the Eden of the future".—**Ingersoll.**

Towards this home of truth in its fullness let us march, with Shankara as the Supreme Commander, may be, and lesser lieutenants in all lands as spiritual echelons. I fondly hope Vachaspati Panoli will lead us to some distance. In the final analysis, Truth is not borrowed or read, repeated or robbed. Authentic experience is the ultimate evidence. Such is the life's message of the acharya who left a legacy and left the terrestrial dimension at young thirty-two!

In solitude and reflective mood, I often feel the essence of an advaidic presence:

"An Intelligence so sublime

Moves behind the scene

The Artist of the Universe

Painting relativity."—Dave Squires

Dear C.K. as you are familiarly known but not fully understood. At four score and three, you are still serving the ailing, not for fee but you regard everyone else as your brother's keeper. In great days the world will understand you fully. Your life is your message. To be misunderstood is itself a sign of greatness in our dark world. I keep you company in this kismet.

> *Is it so bad, then, to be misunderstood? Pythagoras was misunderstood, and Socrates, and Jesus, and Luther, and Copernicus, and Galileo, and Newton, and Marx, and Jesus and Adi Sankara, and every pure and wise spirit that ever took flesh. To be great is to be misunderstood.* **(Emerson)**

May 2, 2009

V.R. Krishna Iyer

1

United We Stand, Divided We Fall

The Indian nation's destiny is shaped by the ballot of the billion and odd voters in a few months under the broad fundamentals of the Constitution. For a culturally Bharat society of several centuries of vintage heritage, you need a stable government, which in turn needs stable parties with basically common manifestoes of national norms under the parameters of the great Constitution. India is a People's Democratic Republic. That is our Panchayat tradition. Nehru explained in the Constituent Assembly this dimension thus: 'I most frankly confess that I am a socialist and a republican, and am no believer in kings or princes or in the order which produces the modern kings of industry, who have greater power over the lives and fortunes of men than even the kings of old, and whose methods are as predatory as those of the old feudal aristocracy. I recognize, however that it may not be possible for a body constituted as it is, the Congress party to adopt a full socialistic programme. But we must realize that the philosophy of socialism has gradually permeated the entire structure of society the world over and almost the only points in dispute are the pace and the methods of advance to its full realization. India will have to go that way, too, if she seeks to end her poverty and inequality, though she may evolve, her own method and may adapt the ideal to the genius of her race.

In short, India was in the Founding Father's vision a socialist, casteless community with a dynamic amity amidst theological pluralism but at bottom is bound by a manifestation of universal divinity in every human. This wonder of oneness must inform our cultural community life in cosmic humanism, illuminate and animate all religions and even the godless atheists. This free patriotic fraternity, celestial spiritual thought, this theological comity and global political vision, are a sine qua non for survival of the large have-not and humble Indian humanity. This deplorable destitute scenario is a horror when we are told by the FAO; 27% poor of the world population is living in India and the richest 4% too are in the same India with 43% of the infant mortality due to meager nourishment and sick privations. No less than 40% of women suffer under-development and masculine domination in social and political power. And food scarcity is not in sight of leaving our weak economy. This sad syndrome is pathetic. Manmohanomics—Chidambaramics—Narasimha Rao's hidden agenda are contradicting our cultural and constitutional values. And yet the governing class in power in the trinity of instrumentalities are oath-bound to uphold a Socialist-Secular-Democratic Republic but betray it by mafia propaganda, class-conscious casteism and using the treacherous trinity of mantras-Globalization, Liberalisation and Privatisation of U.S. mintage, (Dollar Dependencia Syndrome), exotic and native brands in collusion. The philosophers have interpreted the world in various ways. Our task is to transform it, (Marx). Oh! The pity of it, even the Marxists mentally conditioned by industrial glamour have jettisoned Marx. We still behave colonially in our imperial judicial jurisprudence of economic classes in our State's bureaucratic basic structure and micromolar political pluralism and theological rivalry as part of communal casteist pathology and vote-bank strategy to seize power. In such a scenario, socialist-secular egalitarian democracy is illusion and religious unity moonshine, the mafia managing State Power and Gandhi deeply buried in the disguised dimension of development. India lives in its villages which had for ages panchayat democracy. But centralization, crazy for industrialization and the cult of Money over Man, has vulgarized our culture and even gods are after huge money, godmen swindlers and lost in internecine conflict ignoring the development of agriculture but falling victim to fossil, feudal, corrupt, colonial, communal competitive divisiveness and polluting Nature and ideologically hard won swaraj as a fancy five-star mirage. This colonial fraud must change and the village must become vibrant and progressive in the agrarian sphere and not capitulate to capitalist industrialization creating poorly paid wage-earners. The root cause of class and hallowed creamy layers are for luxury life-style, servitude and feudal, colonial pathology projected as five-star development. A new pharmacopoeia synthesisms through a harmony of haves and have-nots through a happy universal humanism, is the socialist vision and mass-oriented mission of our Constitution to win which is our authentic swaraj-*poorna swaraj*. Leftists, you stand by the people, lest people leave you. Yea are salt of Indian earth and if the salt lose their savour, wherewith shall they be salted. We, the People of India united in a finer fraternity - that is Bharat Mahan with Panchayat Raj as the basic democratic unit.

Elections for the 15th Lok Sabha, has electrified the nation into a meaningful militant activism, integrity and fraternity and spell hara-kiri for politicians, left, right and centre. The manifesto of the billion humans is luminously spelt out in the suprema lex as socialist, democratic, secular Republic. But alas, every party - every group or caste from chandala to creamy layer, proletariat to propriateriat, is a fragmented party - has been jettisoned by statesmanship, national vision, united radical passion and abandoned the ideology of the Constitution in favour of ministership, communalism, corruption and terrorism. This must change. Yes, we can. Voters must not sell their soul: but fight for the Constitution. The service of India means the service of the millions who suffer. It means the ending of poverty and ignorance and disease and inequality of opportunity. The ambition of the greatest man of our generation has been to wipe every tear from every eye. That may be beyond us, but as long as there are tears and suffering, so long our work will not be over. The Indian Constitution: Cornerstone of a nation. Indo-Pak non-negotiable friendship, SAARC fraternity, are fundamental if International law of peace and human rights are not to be the vanishing point of Jurisprudence. But even cricket is an opportunity for sermon age and political accusation with Gobbles' audacity and absurdity. Let people of India and

Pakistan come together. The world is sinking. Let us arrest this through honest Swadeshi as the essence of Development which is not of things but of man. Gandhiji said: 'The Gandhian concept of development rejected the idea that it should aim primarily at the creation of material wealth or the satisfaction of insatiable, endlessly multiplied needs'. 'In so far as we have made the modern materialistic craze our goal' he wrote, 'so far we are going downhill in the path of progress.' (The Third World Tomorrow, p. 19).

Today ghostly Gods are Big Business and godmen the new mafia. The Parliamentary Poll pharmacopoeia, the micro-molar melt-down - that is our new grand tryst in this powerful national polls. Today, slum-dog has to sleep hungry in conditions of have-not syndrome and millionaires in luminous palaces. A Swaraj India, you betrayed Gandhi and Nehru and Indira. You the people shall arise, awake and build Bharat Mahan in effective implementation of the Preamble, part II, IV and IVA as fundamental of our great country of egalitarian and humanism and peace in SAARC.

2

Supremacy of Judiciary Fleeting

Indian culture has a supra-materialist dimension which is the basic character of development emphasised in the 42nd Amendment of the Constitution. Indira Gandhi, the then Prime Minister, moved and got it passed stating that the State of India shall be a socialist, secular, democratic Republic. We, the People of India made this tryst on gaining Independence, will make the Prime Minister and the Cabinet liable to removal for unconstitutional conduct. Privatization and economic control through multi-national corporations is a violation of socialist texture of our polity. Although under Westminster and Washington influence, our Prime Minister Narasimha Rao, Manmohan Singh and Chidambaram, the Finance Ministers have been quilty of playing into the hands of American Big Business in the guise of globalization, liberalization and privatization, which are malignant; mantras: violently violative of Gandhian and Nehruvian social philosophy. To ignore agrarian development in favour of borrowed urban industrialization, is contra Gandhian to fill our cities with jungles of concrete skyscrapers and the masses driven into slums and starvation, is a dependence syndrome. With despair for the billion people and rosy freebooter expectations for the billionaires, whose power over Central and State power through new technology and industry is polluting air and water and even outer space. More gluts of motor cars is not prosperity but affluence of a mafia and creamy layer. The country has been made over to the hands of the richer classes. The trinity of instrumentalities, executive, legislative and judicative, have been conditioned to jettison the masses and spiral up the wealth of the higher classes. The have-not humanity of India, which is the real sovereign, will have to struggle to regain swaraj but we have a Government which is living on alcoholic beverages, polluted rivers, foreign investments, imports and proliteriat sans gender justice, pediatric justice, geriatric justice and the right to life in dignity of the vast numbers of Indians who are no longer relevant except some placebos during election time to win vote-banks. Secularism is outraged by the States and Centre in the field of health and education and essentials of life by commercializing these facilities. And the court, strangely, is validating this delinquency by its pronouncements that the people have allergy even to the judiciary; and the executive is pampering and bribing the judiciary by conditioning them with a class-bias. Winston Churchill once said in the U.K. Parliament: "What is valid in India today, our MPs alas are lost in sound and fury signifying nothing and the judiciary itself, if they care to look at themselves in the mirror, will discover broken integrity, insatiable appetite for material wealth."

Let me cite one instance: Four new judges were appointed to the High Court of Marxist Kerala. They were all District Judges and had State cars. They could as well continue the use of these cars if the State Government issues a specific order in that behalf. A financially broken Government, neglecting the public sector, indifferent of prices of essential commodities without controlling them and allowing public finance to be in chaos and surviving on alcohol sales and toxic beverages chose pampering the courts by giving them new Toyota cars, very expensive. But bribery rarely bothers about the value of graft. Nehru insisted for traveling in Ambassador car. So did Indira Gandhi. Perhaps the Marxist party does not believe in swadeshi or economy. Otherwise, they would not have wasted money on Toyota. Why not the Cabinet propitiate the judges by giving Rolls Royce? Let the poor die but the Government will get favourable orders from the High Court by giving fascinating cars and advocate from Delhi to argue their cases in Kochi. Lavish expenditure with no protest in the House! Nehru when informed that 3 days in Madras spent by him as Prime Minister, cost the State Government Rs. 75,000/-, declined to go out of Delhi unless this excessive expenditure was eliminated. When I, as judge of the Supreme Court requested Achutha Menon as Chief Minister to make High Court and Supreme Court judges, State guests, which means free accommodation and free cars, declined because it was avoidable expenditure. Nehru had a sense of economy. The present Government has none. Their T.A. by air is staggering. They are giving 200 litres of petrol per judge, whereas they require not more than 20 litres for official use. None of my colleagues as judge, ever received a single litre free. On the contrary myself, Chinnappa Reddy Judge and Desai Judge minimized the use of gas by taking turns each day to save petrol. The present judges have three free travels every year from one part to the other end of our large country in special class. Judges are offered Rs. 24,000/- per month as rent for houses, while judicial quarters are lying vacant. But the State Government is paying handsome rent for judges continuing in the small houses. Rs. 24,000/- is tax free! The office of the judiciary with these facilities if objectively investigated, would reveal some misappropriation from public finance which brings down the grand institution in the esteem of the people of India. Why do I say all these? Jerome Frank in his book Courts on Trial has given the reason. I quote and conclude:

> "In a democracy, it can ever be unwise to acquaint the public with the truth about the workings of any branch of government. It is wholly undemocratic to treat the public as children who are unable to accept the inescapable shortcomings of man-made institutions...The best way to bring about the elimination of those shortcomings of our judicial system, which are capable of being eliminated, is to have all our citizens informed as to how that system now functions. It is a mistake, therefore, to try to

establish and maintain, through ignorance, public esteem for our courts."

The Central Government is abated in a big way in making the judiciary an ally of the executive by multiplying the salary of judges three times in one stroke. Will the L.D. Clerk of the labouring masses or nurses be given three times their wages? Never, never. Under Manmohanomics in short, we have to fight for the basic structure articulated in Part III and IV of the Constitution. The truth is, the country, India, that is Bharat, no longer belongs to Indians under tradition of Bharat. We had a radical transformation and cultural revision of lifestyle and values to deserve our sovereignty and Gandhi as the Father of the Nation. Yes, we can. If we do not, lawyers will be judges and burnt down police stations. The rule of law must govern rule of life which is to wipe every tear from every eye.

Alas! The judiciary has ceased to be people-oriented. The Bench and the Bar have fallen out and the adversarial system is slowly collapsing. In Madras and Madurai, in the presence of judges a violent fracas took place and judges got stone throw injuries and even beating. What a pity! The cause is deep rooted. Judges must regain their lost esteem. This is a long journey and reminds me of the lines Nehru kept on his table in the Foreign Office :

The woods are lovely, dark, and deep,

But I have promises to keep,
And miles to go before I sleep,
And miles to go before I sleep. (Robert Frost)

The charges of communalism, corruption and other vices freely and openly mentioned about judges is a demand upon judges for good conduct. So I demand a new dynamic Appointment Commission, Performance Commission and constitutional code of conduct for judges. Social justice is not sanguinary jujitsu between the Bench, the Bar and the Police.

3

New Methodology of Selecting Higher Court Judges

A flawsome ruling of the Supreme Court, projected as judicial jurisprudence of dubious noesis, has exaggeratedly created an 'avatar' with power to choose 'justices' as a secret process. Its foundation is an arbitrary doctrine of unfettered independence of the 'robed brethren' of the higher courts, which allegedly absolves them from political, communal and regional partialities, personal angularities, professional anfractuosities, class prejudices and other miscellaneous aberrations. The Judicial Collegium is vested with authority to handpick higher court incumbents, decide on transfers of justices from province to province, and suggest, on their own, elevations to the Supreme Court directly from the Bar or from High Courts. Nothing in the provisions of the long Constitution warrants this bizarre jurisdiction in the Apex Court to invent an extra-ordinary entity, unjustly ignoring the categorical clarification given in the Constituent Assembly by Dr. Ambedkar, Chairman of the Drafting Committee, that only *consultation*, never *concurrence*, would be part of the process of selection of judges. The strange project of an oligarchic collegium is an infantile concept, if I may say so with great respect to our judges generally. This incarnate owes its existence to a pronouncement by a narrow majority of 5 to 4 (Supreme Court Advocates-on-Record Association Vs. Union of India AIR 1994 SC 268) in reversal of a long-standing praxis regarding appointments of judges by the President of India, based on the recommendation of the Central Cabinet. This system has governed since the inception of the Constitution. The Central Executive's proposal constitutionally binds the President. Indeed, great judges of the High Courts and the Supreme Court have been a glory of our Justice System, although appointed by the top executive in consultation with the pro tem Chief Justice of India. The nine judges who sat on the Bench and made the historic upset and spelt out this curious 'collegium' pronouncement themselves were the offspring of the pre-Collegium practice. How, then, did they act with independence? Nowhere in the civilised world have judges themselves seized the power to appoint their own brother (and sister) judges. This unhappy judicial hunger for executive power of a high order is an inglorious departure from the basic structure of the Constitution. Even in Britain, the Lord Chancellor has given up the power of choice of judges and left it to the recommendation of a high-powered committee who included non-judicial statesmen and excluded sitting judicial personalities. It is denial of the democratic process for the people of the country to have no voice in, or even information, about the candidates to be selected for judicial office; the entire operation being usurped, as it were, by an unaccountable Collegium of judges whose decisions are a secrecy, a mystery and an enigma at times. No procedure, no guidelines, no training or discipline, no democracy. Even in the USA where the President has wide powers, there is a critical examination of judicial candidates named by the President, by a senate judiciary sub-committee. This feature is a token of the people's right to know. The basic principle of natural justice which must apply to judicial appointments, is aptly expressed in an ancient Roman adage "Whatever touches us all should be decided by all". Transparency and accountability are rules of natural justice. It follows that the people's representatives must have a direct or indirect opportunity to express their views on the appointment of judges.

The judicial invention of the contraption of Collegium as instrument for selection of judges, consisting of the three senior-most judges of the High Court concerned, at the initial stage, and the seniormost three judges of the Supreme Court at the final stage is imposing at first sight but unscientific, impractical and unfair, viewed objectively. Selection from among a large number of advocates summons skills in scrutiny of the merits of candidates. Three judges, accidentally the senior-most, possess no special training; nor have they any criteria made out for testing the capacity of the candidates. Three lay persons, who may be good judges in hearing cases, are raw hands when functioning as selecting agency without guidelines or public consultation with the Bar or with other judges, on the professional merits, character and integrity, social philosophy, political commitments and other factors of relevance, including class and religion;

makes the operation odd, even arbitrary. On the contrary, a large number of advocates of High Court Bar and excellent lawyers from the mofussil have no chance of being considered for judgeship. Trial lawyers are ignored altogether. Specialization in various branches of law may have no relevance if the three top judges, who constitute the selection committee, are ignorant of particular branches of jurisprudence. Moreover, partiality, relationship to judges, dynastic factors, high income, caste and community considerations, prevail in many cases. There should be publicity in the process of selection. The names of candidates under active consideration must be known to the public. Then favourable and unfavourable aspects, relevant to the candidate's plus and minus *vis-a-vis* his judgeship may be brought to the notice of the Collegium by social activists, advocates, jurists and others. The Administration may have their views on the candidates. Currently, they have no voice nor opportunity for communication. The Collegium does not investigate into antecedents and social background of candidates nor has any facilities for it and is not accountable to any other body or administrative machinery. Even the bar has no formal information about the candidates under consideration. The whole process is almost privatized, personalized and ignorant of governmental comments. Whispers and rumours prevalent; through the media, manipulations, friendships and partialities go a long way. More failings and fallibilities can be added to the inadequacy of the Collegium as an instrumentality. Persons are chosen, privileged groups get priority, reconsideration is often rejected. The Collegium has an unscientific methodology and its selection has given rise to much criticism. The Law Minister at the Centre once expressed criticism of the system, but now, with the life of parliament over, the Government gave up any change which requires constitutional amendment. Weaknesses are writ large in this judicial engineering. Therefore, the Collegium, as a system, must go. What next?

If appointments of judges are not to suffer the syndrome of disappointments, if the selection of the members of the higher tribunals of the nation are to comply with the sensitive technology of socialist, secular democracy, if egalitarian opportunity is to be open for all candidates with potential excellence, if investigation into the merits of candidates from various relevant sources is to be a condition for the elevation of advocates to the Bench, if transparency, accountability and exposure of proposed nominees to public criticism through responsible information, imparted confidentially to the appointing agency is fair, then we need a constitutional code, comprehensive and principled, laying down the jurisprudence of judicial selection so that the justice system may command the reverence of the country. The accidental Collegium elitism is the vanishing point of democratic values in the Justice Pyramid.

4

Veil of Secrecy over Judiciary Mars Fundamentals

Beware of the embryonic incarnation of a 'robed' trade union born with a material tendency springing from the insatiable addiction to 'West is best' craze. The curial Robe, traditionally worn on the Bench by the British 'brethren', is a noble symbol of a learned profession with royal authority - the glorious judiciary. This august apparel has enjoyed the constitutional halo in 'Colonial India' of Judge Power, and enchanting popular esteem vis-a-vis the lofty status and stature of an 'independent' authority - all because this elite instrumentality consists of a select fine fraternity endowed with vast legal powers and enjoys, as a 'lordly' community, a sublime reputation and confidence, fair and rare, fearless and far aloof as a glowing oligarchy. This glorious group is expected to be incorruptibly above purchase, pollution or pleasure from any quarter, executive or other. Never departing from their sacred commitment to unadulterated administration of justice, this hallowed sector functions, superlatively from the floor trial level to a spiral up-to apex national deck. Ever transparent and impartial between citizens, high and humble, free from pride or prejudice, arrogance, arbitrariness or authoritarian hauteur but acting with socialist egalite and secular sensitivity in strict compliance with the Constitution and the laws. The judicature is geared to the grant of relief and imposition of penalty with forward functional simplicity, behavioural dignity, decency, decorum and democratic accountability in conduct, public or private. Judges are judges on or off the Bench. Do you know Justice Douglas issued an interim writ stopping Vietnam bombing from his home? Why no American shall die nor kill by aggression without Congress sanction? *Fiat Justicia*, in this grand semantic humanism, is too hallowed a temple of *social service* which deserves to be honoured nationally and commands high patriotic honour, on and off the Bench. The first priority on a judge's agenda is his status as national fiduciary with constitutional obligations. This is hard to practice, but is a must in observance. Never depart from this lofty standard and don't taint the hallowed judiciary from this superlative, straight-forward lifestyle of *moral majesty*. How gracious and glorious is this great judicial profession! But this credential grandeur is forfeited if judges jettison the public values which are integral to the robe. Never rob it of its valiant virtues until you retire from office and even as a retired judge, don't stultify the splendid fraternity to which you belonged and hunger for lucre. Never bid farewell to your Past. Every public servant who wields power over another, inarticulately but inexorably, subjects himself to this severe conditionality. Why? Because all power is a trust which springs from the people and is accountable to the people in a Democratic Republic. This is *a fortiori* applicable to the judiciary for the obvious reason that higher the power, graver the responsibility to Indian humanity. The jurisprudence of power makes no exception in favour of the 'robed brethren'. Late Justice Douglas, a great American judge, observed in general terms what we, in India, may apply to those who operate judicial power and myopically seek and make themselves an exception. "...all power tends to develop into a government in itself. Power that controls the economy should be in the hands of elected representatives of the people, not in the hands of an industrial oligarchy. Industrial power should be decentralized. It should be scattered into many hands so that the fortunes of the people will not be dependent on the whim or caprice, the political prejudices, the emotional stability of a few self-appointed men. The fact that they are not vicious men but respectable and social-minded is irrelevant". Emphatically, this basic ethos with a people-orientation must govern the court's power engineers. In this context, the remarkable book 'The Brethren', a daring, veracious U.S. publication, may be read profitably. It is amazing that so many unhappy but authentic secrets about the Apex Judges of the Washington - inmates of the marble marvel - are disclosed. The radiant robes of the Bhagwandas Road in Delhi must submit themselves to public scrutiny. Yes, if you want to hide, be you ever so high, better be out. Our judges need to be clean, like those of the USA who have been revealed without hesitation. No jurist or court thought of contempt action against me. Chief Justice Warren Burger quoted in the book, is apt here. "In a country like ours, no public institution, or the people who operate it, can be above debate". A few Indian judicial cowards, with a pusillanimous community complex, may not agree. Have courage or surrender your robe! Remember, a judge is not a cloistered virtue but a public functionary whose activities are above board, open to democratic visibility, amenable to responsible invigilation. 'Contempt for a question prior to investigation, prevents all progress and keeps man in eternal ignorance' (Herbert Spencer – Quote It-II p. 95).

Under our Constitution, freedom of expression is a fundamental right. Free speech, reasonable and responsible, necessarily involves free access to information which is the basis of fair expression. Therefore, when public conduct or private asset or other feature affecting societal affairs of a public servant, including a judicial officer, high or low, is involved and forms the subject of expression, the right to information, which is basic to free expression, itself is integral to the fundamental right, guaranteed in Article 19, of free speech. Corruption is almost ubiquitous; so too women-related vices. These can be extirpated only by exposure. Accumulation of disproportionate wealth, erotic escapades and other covert freebooting operations and even sex excess, can and must be brought to light even in the case of judges and ministers and secretaries and this can be done *only* if these materials are not hidden but are, *as of right*, made available to responsible social activists, not of course, to frivolous or reckless busybodies. Broad secrecy is the hidden enemy of people's *right to know*. It follows that 'the right to know' which vests in every Indian citizen vis a vis public servants cannot be nullified by any jejune mask of judicial office. There exists no iron curtain under Indian jurisprudence between a person's search for information about the assets and a public servant's wealth. Be he any public servant even if he be a judge of the higher court. Bribery, graft and myriad malignant and miscellaneous misbehaviours and aberrations are growing in our country with rapidity and this grave escalation has made no exception in the case of one who wears a robe as a judicial official or as a religious functionary. The robe can never rob truth and justice nor screen from view roguery and rascality from the solar light of public interest scrutiny. Indeed, the Freedom of Information Act (FOI Act) did not create the Right to Information for the first time. That right existed under the Constitution and even under the law governing fiduciary functionaries and others with similar powers and responsibilities. Democracy is people's vicarious right of governance which obligates power-wielders to act publicly. The Freedom of Information Act created a viable machinery for easier enforcement of the right to know. The irresistible conclusion is that the judges, executive echelons and all those who exercise public power are above the plea of secrecy and under a duty to disclose. 'Satyameva jayate' is our non-negotiable logo and paramount mandate of public power. India, true to constitutional rectitude, can be clean only when public official's purses, bank balances and other forms of property are an open book. If judges can be secret and safe pickpockets and immune to disclosure, our justice system will suffer the pathology of unearned wealth, covert bribery, illicit accumulations and abundance of benami estates, with no therapy of truth to cure this versatile rape syndrome. If the law blinks at the duty to unfold a public officer's financial balloon, the rule of law collapses in its battle against plundering mafia.

This shall not be. Justice, social, economic and political, become brash and vain verbiage if judges, oath-bound, defeat the suprema lex. The moment the President of India, the Prime Minister of India, the Chief Justice of India, the CAG of India and the top echelons of the Defence Forces and different departments and the vast spiral of bureaucrats gain the legal right to secrete illicit wealth and myriad misconduct from public know-how with valid immunity, the law of the barbarian, the law of the jungle takes over and democracy dwindles and value-viable jurisprudence reaches vanishing point or low nadir. Such a national casualty *we shall overcome. Yes, we can.* A self-created secrecy, as a professional privilege, even if expounded rashly by the high judiciary, smacks of bizarre trade unionism. This exclusion from freedom of information is violative of the majestic reputation of sterling constitutional guarantor of human rights. Judges are humans and not angels. Failings and temptations are not alien to their cadres. In the classic phrases of Justice Black of the U.S. Supreme Court in Green vs. United States (356 U.S 165 198): 'Judges are not essentially different from other government officials. Fortunately they remain human even after assuming their judicial duties. Like all the rest of mankind they may be affected from time to time by pride and passion, by pettiness and bruised feelings, by improper understanding or by excessive zeal.' (Quote It-I p.299)

Listen to Justice Frankfurter: 'Judges as persons, or courts as institutions, are entitled to no greater immunity from criticism than other persons or institutions. Just because the holders of judicial office are identified with the interests of justice they may forget their common human frailties and fallibilities. There have sometimes been martinets upon the bench as there have also been pompous wielders of authority who have used the paraphernalia of power in support of what they called their dignity. Therefore judges must be kept mindful of their limitations and of their ultimate public responsibility by a vigorous stream of criticism expressed with candor however blunt.' (Quote It-I pp. 286/287)

Judges occupy a high pedestal in public life. Their conduct has to maintain a high standard of excellence as implied in the Constitution itself. The behavioural optimum of the '*brethren*' (why, sisters too), has been the subject of national discussion. Our judges themselves, at the Supreme Court and High Court levels, ultimately in 1997 arrived at a unanimous code, brief but precise, which was accepted on the administrative side by the Chief Justices of the High Courts and by the judges of the Supreme Court. This includes the obligation of judges to present to the Chief Justice of India a statement of their assets. Such a revelation is not for fun or joke or an idle paper tiger or for the meditation of fleeting Chief Justices of India. It is a fulfillment of the onus, celestial to communicate to the socialist people of India, the assets of judges. The code of conduct, in my view, may be made part of the Constitution as a schedule called the Code of Behaviour of the Judges of Higher Courts. It is a happy omen that the former Chief Justice Verma insists that the assets of the judges, although confidentially kept by the Chief Justice of India, is public information under the Freedom of Information Act available to all social activists or solemn persons responsibly in search of the conduct and delinquencies of judicial personnel. So be it. Secrecy leads to suspicion. The great agnostic and celebrated lawyer of the United States, Robert Ingersoll, once observed: 'suspicion is the Upas tree under whose shade reason fails and justice dies. Let us place our judges, like Caesar's wife, above suspicion.'

5

Supreme Court cannot Grab Constitution

Supreme Court is not final and nor infallible but must function under the Constitution, otherwise the court must be packed as F.D. Roosevelt proposed for indiscipline and liability to be impeached. And yet the highest Bench sets up six fast track courts. This is functional excess and the Executive must ignore it as a direction, not carry it out as a writ. The basic structure of our Constitution is Montesquian - the trinity of the Administration being Executive, Legislative and Judicative. The court cannot usurp this inviolable tracheotomy of functional iron curtain. Unelected arbitrary judicial excess or aberration is robed tyranny and unconstitutional terror which destroys our democracy and people's voice in Administration. If the court can appoint more judges to liquidate arrears in the Supreme Court itself, that is a deficiency which desiderates changes of lazy judges on the highest Bench as the snail's pace disposals and frequent travels is not restricted or streamlined the professional output of work by judges themselves.

True, our Founding Fathers gave considerable

powers to the higher judges but every one derives authority *under* the Constitution not *over* it. The fundamental design in Montesquian and what belongs to the executive, cannot be usurped by the judicative. Otherwise, we will produce chaos of the Constitution and the country's governance will become a dysfunctional anarchy. Appointment of other judges is not a judicial function because they do not have the equipment or the guidelines or the training or the investigative machinery for selecting the best personnel or even to ascertain available candidates far away from Delhi in a provincial bar. The order to appoint six fast track courts is regrettably an arbitrary departure from adjudicative operations. All that I can say from Parkinson's Law and Peter Principle, the first rule is an abuse and the second one incompetence. In short, I would suggest forthwith for the robbed brethren involved to direct immediate action to the Executive. Give directions to the Government to appoint under specific guidelines but not do what another instrumentality alone is entitled to do.

Good judges, poor scholars, poorer administrators, when they wrest authority for sheer pleasure of exercise of appointments, soon prove disappointments because of Parkinson's Law and Peter Principle. Redundant and incompetent judges fill the Bench and the remedy aggravates the melody of delay and disastrous arrears. To wind up my comments with great respect to the hallowed high Bench it is necessary for every agency under the Constitution to realize the scope of its power and limitations so that to know oneself is the first patriotic duty of every functionary under the constitutional law. God himself should not become almighty belligerent, lest the world gets deep in blood by war. In Ingersoll's words; 'An honest God is the noblest work of man'. So too an honest man is the noblest work of God. This applies to judges as well.

6

Judges are not Comrades-in-Arms

If Indian judicature is not to suffer degeneration as a caricature, democracy must assert itself and it must cease to be a simulacrum of royal Westminster judges with jacket and robed apparel.

Let no dubious doctrine be invented to bride the Bench into immunized corruption. Glasnost and perestroika, with an Indian genius will grant our Judicature a rare stature. But, alas, it is like a new class of godmen in all religions, who have turned criminals. Though of a secular fraternity, they have shed robes of their sacred probity, at least in micro measure through a gradually growing, traumatic trade unionism, which is anathema to justice as a value, justices as a profession and justicing as a process.

The grandeur of the Indian Judicary has been marred by another enigmatic factor. I am not referring to any phenomenon of judicial terrorism. True, a few judges go off the balance, behave bedlam fashion and unblushingly give the impression of corruption, communalism and family favouritism directly or indirectly. Fortunately this evil is confined to a tiny fraction. This menace can be eliminated by a performance Commission of a high order which I have advocated more than once. The trade unionist feature of capturing executive power by pressure, is manifest in another way. The process is innocent but in my view unwarranted by the Constitution. I refer to the colloqulum phenomenon based on the pronouncement of a nine Judge Bench which held, by a narrow majority of one, that the independence of the judiciary demands the taking over of the selection of judges of the Higher Courts by a batch of three seniormost judges. The executive power of appointment of judges is wrested from the Cabinet and is exercised by a judicial colloquium.

The great judge Douglas (U.S. Supreme Court) said: '...the law of contempt is not made for the protection of judges who may be sensitive to the winds of public opinion. Judges are supposed to be men of fortitude, able to thrive in a hardy climate.' (Quote It-I p. 284)

Where is the testimony of hijacking the hallowed judiciary into Trade Unionism? Here are a few instances which make out a prima facie case (1) Judges work only for: 180 days in the highest court and 210 days in the High Court. The pendency of old cases is staggeringly mounting and dilatory disposals aggravate the ghastly arrears. But the courts do not care to abolish long vacations or reduce long travels taking leave merrily. But our egalitarian judges are willing to hear proprietary cases even on Sundays or late hours at night vide Harrison Malayalam Ltd case on Sunday staying an order of the State against the MNC. (2) Some judges laze leisurely and take days of hearing, and granting easy adjournments where another hour or two would have been sufficient to close the case.

Procrastination and precipitancy are unbecoming of Judges. Indolence and garrulous extravagance on the Bench is not unusual. Arrogance and ignorance cannot but be criticized. But there is no disciplinary guidelines nor supervisory vigilance whatever, over dawdling judicialese. (3) Some judges attend weddings and other diversions including cricket matches and other games during court time with none to call them to order. (4) Where instant hearings and prompt disposals are possible for diligent judges, performance is perfunctory, judgments are delayed by days, months and, alas years! Why? There is no performance audit. (5) There are judges, some senior or are even Chief Justices who do not deliver judgments at all. Shocking, but there is no punitive jurisdiction or alternative instruments of enquiry. No judgments delivered - an alarming failure; but yet they get promotion or elevation to the highest court. Judges of the Supreme Court also share, though rarely, these failings because there is no code of conduct nor Performance Commission with penal jurisprudence (6) Judges have no behavioural propriety and so many courts suffer from functional anarchy. (7) Here is a new proposition in an undemocratic assertion of absolute independence. Forensic accountability has suffered solar eclipse. They may be guilty of bribery, benami acquisition, disproportionate wealth, expensive alcoholism and yet they demand immunity and secrecy beyond the law and above other citizens sheltered by a bizarre iron curtain from revelation or disclosure. To gag expression of disapproval of judicial delinquency is to guillotine free speech, a fundamental right. (8) In our greedy age, culture has become commercial and the judges in a display of high power, demand a dramatic escalation of remuneration even as labour asks for more wages when the economy is sick and the common people suffer unemployment. Another feature of the higher judiciary which smacks of trade unionism, a hunger to secure more place pride of in the community, is the increase in salary. India has a large population of have-nots, handicapped and plural deprivation of human rights. The most prominent of which is the right to life and dignity guaranteed as a fundamental right under Article 21 of the Constitution. The judges of the High Courts and the Supreme Courts have by a single stroke of the executive ensure to keep the court in good humour by multiplying the salary of judges three times forgetting that a depression has gripped the country's economy and unemployment is escalating itself three times. To cover up this injustice, implicit in fabulous increase of salaries shared by the judges with the trade unions, the judges are asking for more emolument and perks doing less work, creating more arrears and more jobs for judges according to Parkinsons' Laws and inevitably with Peter Principle which ensure incompetence and inefficient in the higher echelons of the judiciary. Curiously, the Supreme Court has the photographs of the judges who have no accountability for aggravation of arrears of cases. Their photographs were displayed in public perhaps for the people of a county to know who are the guilty parties who have to answer for the staggering pendency of arrears defeating the right to justice of the common Indian. When public criticism identified culpable judges and voiced their concern the photographs were removed but public memory will not crash by the presentation or withdrawal of photographs. The infinite facts remain that judges have lost their conscience because of curious sense of Independence without accountability. These two values go together and it is absolutely important that trade union tactics will not salvage the judges. The quality of justicing has to change and a social philosophy which involves transformation of the basic structure of the judiciary tuned to distressing the status of public finance is consummation devoutly to be wished.

I may reinforce my submission of truth about the public and private life of the learned members of the Bench by quoting the famous statement of Judge Jerome Frank: "In a democracy, it can ever be unwise to acquaint the public with the truth about the workings of any branch of government. It is wholly undemocratic to treat the public as children who are unable to accept the inescapable shortcomings of man-made institutions...The best way to bring about the elimination of those shortcomings of our judicial system which are capable of being eliminated is to have all our citizens informed as to how that system now functions. It is a mistake, therefore, to try to establish and maintain, through ignorance, public esteem for our courts."

May I beseech the finer members of the fraternity of the judiciary to appreciate that it is in the sublime interest of the Indian Republic and, in particular, the resplendent 'robed' community to ensure that the splendid standards of moral values and ethos of excellence are sustained, commanding, as ever, the marvelous majesty of the curial instrumentality.

Let us not permit misinterpreting by some Chief Justice or constitutional benches of high courts to ruin this great reputation, by privatizing or concealment of information. Justice Douglas, whom I regard as among the greatest judges of the English speaking world, fearlessly opened himself to executive opposition by staying the bombing of Vietnam as a vacation judge, although his order of stay was reversed by a Division Bench. It is worthwhile reading from "The Brethren" about Justice Douglas. (p. 278/279).

"Douglas agreed to hold a hearing on the request and travelled fifty miles down from the foothills of the Cascades to the courthouse in Yakima, Washington.

The government's attorney suggested that a confrontation should be avoided.

"We live in a world of confrontations," Douglas replied. "That's what the whole system is about. I don't enjoy these confrontations myself. I'd rather be up at Goose Prairie."

After the hearing Douglas decided to end the Court of Appeals' stay. The district court could then proceed to order a bombing halt. It was already late in the afternoon and Douglas phoned the Court in Washington to leave word that the printers should not go home. He dictated the first part of the opinion from a truck stop on the way to Goose Prairie. "Do you have that?" he asked. His secretaries struggled to hear him over the din of trucks in the background. The exchange was repeated again from another phone as he proceeded down the road. He read the last section from Whistlin' Jacks, the final rest stop, and last public telephone, before Goose Prairie.

Douglas compared the case to a capital punishment case :

> "The classic capital case is whether Mr. Lew, Mr. Low, or Mr. Lucas should die. The present case involved whether Mr. X (an unknown person or persons) should die. No one knows who they are. They may be Cambodian farmers whose only "sin" is a desire for socialized medicine to alleviate the suffering of their families and neighbors. Or Mr. X may be the American pilot or navigator who drops a ton of bombs on a Cambodian village. The upshot is that we know that someone is about to die.

"Since denial of the application before me would catapult our airmen as well as Cambodian peasants into the death zone, I do what I think any judge would do in a capital case."

Dougla's order and opinion were filed at the Supreme Court the next morning, August 4. The government immediately went back to Marshall, asking him to prevent the district court's order halting the bombing from going into effect.

Marshall found himself in a dilemma. Normally a single Justice would never overrule another. It was one thing to act when another Justice had refused. But once an order had been issued by a Justice, it was up to the full conference to decide whether to reverse it.

The judicature is too great a public instrument to sink as a caricature because one or two myopic Chief Justices seek to hide from public vision. When I staged or declined *absolute* stay of Indira Gandhi's election as M.P., I never, surrendered to fear or favour but performed my public duty and survived executive indignation although a great calamity as Emergency which followed my order was upheld by a larger Bench with Chief Justice Ray and Judges Chandrachud and Bhagwathi.

To sum up, the court is not a covert conspiracy but eloquently open and fearlessly frank. Secrecy is incompatible with the judiciary; otherwise our democracy will become a travesty and the have-not humanity will be under an authoritarian governance by a proprietary oligarchy. This shall not be since our Republic is people's power not 'riddle wrapped in a mystery inside an enigma'. Today, having spent well over seven years of the best part of my life in the Supreme Court of India to make it the Supreme Court for Indians, I must resist every tendency which reduces the confidence of the Indian people in the Indian judiciary, which still has a high place in our society because 'Never in the field of human conflict was so much owed by so many to so few.' (Winston Churchill – Oxford Quotations, p. 150).

7

Humane Judge : An Unceasing Stardom in Any System

It was the boast of Augustus that he found Rome of brick and left it of marble. But now much nobler will be the sovereign's boast when he shall have it to say that he found law dear and left it cheap; found it a sealed book and left it a living letter; found it the patrimony of the rich and left it the inheritance of the poor; found it the two-edged sword of craft and oppression and left it the staff of honesty and the shield of innocence. **(Henry Peter)**

How glorious our generation if we can create a transformation of the legal system to facilitate Humane Judges to survive the current global collapse of moral syndrome.

It was the boast of Gandhi and Nehru who found *Law India* of imperial Victorian vintage and won independent India and left it a socialist secular democratic Republic. Shall we betray this great transformation, by treaty with Israel and colonial subordination to President Bush?

How supreme is our generation which has had the glorious opportunity of liberation from Victorian imperial domination of the Indian empire by Crown and Commons and inauguration of Free Bharat or

Sovereign Swaraj without violence and war, and installed in the might prone throne of the Viceroy, the Governor General and eventually, the Rashtrapathi of India in Rashtrapathi Bhavan! It is the boast of 'We, the People of India' to behold the tricolour flag fly aloft with the Union Jack having been respectfully brought down forever, the previous night as we sang in patriotic chorus the National Anthem sung with nationalist vibrancy as the Constitution declares India a Sovereign Democratic Republic.

Dear Sisters and Brothers of the Commonwealth judicial fraternity be proud we are makers of the majesty of Bharat Mahan in Law and Life.

In this brave background, I am deeply grateful to the Indian Association of Senior Advocates for having invited me for inaugurating a Seminar on 'The Human Judge'. This is a peculiar, profound philosophical proposition at once embracing and enigmatic and too bizarre for me because I am not a senior advocate and too humble to claim the credentials of a human judge. Then how and why did I submit to this puzzle-some mystery? So, it requires a statement of the background in which this seemingly celestial wizard but berserk proposition happens to be put on me, when it is otherwise a riddle wrapped in a mystery. Therefore, I am least qualified to paint the compassionate profile of a human judge. Of course, I am a humane member of the Indian judiciary and have devoted my life for a slew cause of global, humanist and social justice. Indeed, one of my mottos in life, Republic Day greetings is 'I am a human; I count nothing pertaining to humans is alien to me!' By this dimension I am a human judge but much more meaning is packed into the brief but luminous expression *human judge*. Unfortunately, this species of compassionate wing of the judiciary is vanishing, rare and on the verge of extinction. But the judiciary in its high glory can never agree to a downhill process. We will fight on and survive. Sans humanity, Justice stands seppuku. We will struggle to survive. Nevertheless, it is the glorious Bar, a nidus to generate an instrumentality of justice.

A Great Bar the Nidus of A Noble Judicature

It is indispensable and inconceivable that human judges cannot suffer eclipse so long as the Indian Bar holds high its finest blossom a Human Judge as its lovely product. Back to the beginning, who is a truly kindly robed brethren? *Who is a human judge?* Not in the material or lexical sense alone but in the spiritual, moral kindliest sense and honest semantics as well. The best answer comes from that cyclonic sadhu Swami Vivekananda who was a towering personality in the East and the West and the champion of the paraya and pulaya of have-not humanity and the princely sector of the creamy layer of the higher hierarchy of the huge feudal Indian community at large who constitute 'We, the People of India'. I have quoted him later in this paper. But the puzzle remains - baffling theme this majestic how did I get into this mystery? The answer is a letter to me from Sri. Krishnamani:

Dated 7th February 2009

Respected Sir,

Sub. : Function to felicitate you and to have a talk by you in our conference.

"You will be glad to know that recently I was requested to be the chairman of all India Senior Advocates' Forum under the Bar Association of India. This All India Senior Advocates' Forum wants to hold a function in Ernakulam to felicitate you for your yeoman contribution as a great judge and as a great judge and as a great personality and to have a Seminar on "Human Judge – do we have him?", where you will be the main speaker. Sri Fali Nariman, President of Bar Association of India, Sri. Anil Diwan, future President of Bar Association of India and Sri Lalit Bhasin Secretary General of Bar Association of India will also participate in the function. We have chosen Ernakulam only to suit your convenience.

"You may kindly indicate 2 or 3 dates convenient to you preferably in March or April 2009 so that we can choose one of them and print the invitation card accordingly, after informing you of the date. If the date chosen is a Saturday or Sunday it will be more convenient to the advocates' community and convenient for us also to go over there.

"Kindly intimate us of the dates convenient to you so that we can make further arrangements."

My Reply

March 19, 2009

Dear Sri. Krishnamani,

"I have received your letter sent through Sri. Kylasanatha Pillay asking me to participate in a seminar on behalf of the Senior Advocates of India to be organized in Kochi on a date suitable to me preferably on the dates mentioned in the letter or on Saturdays or Sundays in April on an odd subject "Human Judge – do we have him". I am still in a mystery as to the flattery involved in your celebrating National Conference as a tribute to me. Be that as it may. We may hold the meeting on 18th April 2009 one of the dates indicated by you as suitable to Senior Advocates of Delhi. After the date is accepted and fixed, please give the details of your acceptance, the time and the expected subject you want me to speak on and the length of time I can rob from the valuable time of Senior Advocates of India."

With warmest wishes,

Yours sincerely,

(V.R. Krishna Iyer)

To

Sri. M.N. Krishnamani

Senior Advocate
Supreme Court of India
"SARAYU", K-10A Kailash Colony
New Delhi-110 048

Dated 24th March 2009

Dear and Respected Sir,

I read your letter. Thank you for agreeing to 18th April 2009.

"This National Meet is arranged by Bar Association of India through its wing "All India Senior Advocates Forum" for which I happen to be the Chairman.

"We are expecting 10 to 15 Senior Advocates and other leading advocates to attend the function. Apart from me, Sri Lalit Bhasin and Sri Prashant, the following leading Senior Advocates have agreed to participate in the function:

1. Sri. Fali S. Nariman
2. Sri. K.K. Venugopal

3. Sri. P.P. Rao
4. Sri. Anil Diwan
5. Sri. Andiyarjina
6. Sri Gopal Subramaniam

"We will be inviting lawyers from Cochin-Bar. We will also be inviting all the High Court Judges and retired Supreme Court and retired High Court Judges in Kerala to the function. The main object of the function is two-fold :

"I. To honour you for your great and matchless contribution in the field of law and in giving a new meaning to Art. 14 and Art. 21 by adopting a dynamic approach to Constitutional Interpretation with common-man as the focus.

"II. To have a discourse by you on the topic:

"The Human Judge."

This was decided since we all feel that there is lack of justice-oriented approach and compassion in our judges and since we all feel that judicial activism and concept of PIL are not, of late serving the purpose originally intended. We feel that law will remain dry law and unless it is tempered with compassion, it will never transform into Justice.

We want from you as to how an ideal judge should behave and function and as to where we are going wrong in not being in a position to get good and brilliant judges and as to: Why this system has not produced another V.R. Krishna Iyer?

We want to take a full video coverage of your speech and to depict it in different States later by organizing Seminars in the background of your speech. The intention is to bring about awareness about the requirements in an ideal judge.

I think I have answered the queries raised in your letter. If any more clarification is required I will be too happy to respond to the same.

With regards,

Yours sincerely,

(M.N. Krishnamani)

The Bench at its luminous best emerges from the Bar in its finer lawyers and so necessary, a consequential interrogation springs to my mind. Who is a human Advocate? Is he available now? I confess at the beginning, I am not one and cannot boast of being one.

Among the good judgments relevant to the subject is my last opinion pronounced on the last day of my office where I have glanced at this topic reported in 1981 1 SCC 246. Jurisprudence is in one sense social engineering and has a philosophical foundation of the universal human quality, socialism, secularism and democracy. This is the structural basic of our constitution as projected by our Founding Fathers. Three score years of independence have passed by and our first great Prime Minister Jawaharlal Nehru believed in the above principles. He was agnostic theologically, humanist and socialist by the philanthropic standard of cosmic compassion for all lovely, living creatures, and tirelessly strove to build a world of peaceful coexistence and an India of unity, integrity and fraternity, comity among nations and the

Fundamental Rights of freedom of faith, liberty and worship and fundamental duties of fraternity for all living beings and respect for the sublime heritage articulated in 51A :

(*a*) to abide by the Constitution and respect its ideals and institutions, the National Flag and the National Anthem;

(*b*) to cherish and follow the noble ideals which inspired our national struggle for freedom;

(*c*) to uphold and protect the sovereignty, unity and integrity of India;

(*d*) to defend the country and render national service when called upon to do so;

(*e*) to promote harmony and the spirit of common brotherhood amongst all the people of India transcending religious, linguistic and regional or sectional diversities; to renounce practices derogatory to the dignity of women;

(*f*) to value and preserve the rich heritage of our composite culture;

(*g*) to protect and improve the natural environment including forests, lakes, rivers and wild life, and to have compassion for living creatures;

(*h*) to develop the scientific temper, humanism and the spirit of inquiry and reform;

(*i*) to safeguard public property and to abjure violence;

(*j*) to strive towards excellence in all spheres of individual and collective activity so that the nation constantly rises to higher levels of endeavour and achievement.

(*k*) Who is a parent or guardian, to provide opportunities for education to his child or, as the case may be, ward between the age of six and fourteen years.

The cultural quintessence of our Constitutional conscience is provided on the unique upanishadic philosophy of 'Adwaita' a cosmic wonder of global glory as superbly explained by Vivekananda:

"Unity in variety is the plan of the universe. We are all men and yet we are all distinct from one another. As a part of humanity, I am one with you and as Mr So-and-so I am different from you. As a man you are separate from the woman; as a human being you are one with the woman. As a man you are separate from the animal, but as living beings, man, woman, animal, and plant, are all one; and as existence, you are one with the whole universe. That universal existence is God, the Ultimate Unity in the universe. In Him we are all one. At the same time, in manifestation, these differences must always remain. In our work, in our energies, as they are being manifested outside, these differences must always remain. We find then that if by the idea of a universal religion, it is meant that one set of doctrines should be believed by all mankind, it is wholly impossible. It can never be, there can never be a time when all faces will be the same. Again if we expect, that there will be one universal mythology, that is also impossible, it cannot be. Neither can there be one universal ritual. Such a state of things can never come into existence; if it ever did, the world would be destroyed, because variety is the first principle of life. What makes us formed beings? Differentiation. Perfect balance would be our destruction. Suppose the amount of heat in this room, the tendency of which is towards equal and perfect diffusion, gets that kind of diffusion, then for all practical purposes that heat will cease to be. What makes motion possible in this universe? Lost balance. The unity of sameness can come only when this universe is destroyed, otherwise such a thing is impossible. Not only so, it would be dangerous to have it. We must not wish that all of us should think alike. There would then be no thought to think. We should be all alike, as the Egyptain mummies in a museum, looking at each other without a thought to think. It is this difference, this differentiation, this losing of a balance between us, which is the very soul of our progress, the soul of all our thought. This must always be." (Words of Wisdom from Swami Vivekananda)

And eclectic liberalism at its universal acme is in the Rigveda:

Let noble thoughts come to us from every side.

Is A Human Judge Or Human Attorney Available Now?

No Human Advocate, no human Judge. So let us search for the humanist advocate. Is a Human Judge current coin? Is that species extant or extinct? I can recollect only of one human advocate - Mahatma Gandhi, or Abraham Lincoln both world famous for their inviolable commitment to life in dignity and Truth total for truth and principled non-violence. In India when Gandhi practiced as a lawyer, he had hardly begun as a lawyer. Then he shifted to South Africa where he had large practice. He was a fearless nationalist and stood for dignity and humanism although the Bench before which he appeared was European and dark Africa itself was constantly under the domination of the Whites in culture and ways of life. Gandhiji even in those young days was an uncompromising idealist under the benign influence of

Tolstoy and Thoreau. He was an unusual lawyer who put his principle into professional practice. So, he insisted on certain imperatives when clients approached him. He was a barrister scrupulous on two non-negotiable points. He would extract two promises from his clients. Firstly, he claimed freedom to get to know the whole truth of the case adverse or favourable to his client and these were the facts that he would tell the court only the truth and nothing but the truth; mindless of whether it was adverse to his client's interest or not. Second principle he made mandatory was, his right to accept what struck him as a fair compromise without consulting his client. Not litigative victory but just settlement was his aim of social justice. Only then he would appear in the case. After a time his reputation for these inflexible values impressed the Bar and the Bench. So much so, after Gandhi had stated his facts, the Bench would accept it as the truth and limited arguments of the counsel on the other side not to cover the fact - which they accepted from Gandhi's statement and confined the opposition only to argue on the law and fair compromises he would readily accept. This created a new splendid reputation of Gandhi as a lawyer. He has claimed that sticking to the truth, more clients were willing to come to him. His practice flourished and his lucrative income despite his unhappy disclosure of unfavourable truth did not suffer decline even by a rupee. This was the last of *human* attorneys at the Bar. But today's judges clamour for more salaries. Judges drawing a salary of Rs. 4,000/- a month earlier now are paid 80,000/-, avaricious inflation and expensive perks. More judgments were delivered by me in 7 years than any other judge for a comparable period. Judges demand latest model cars, change them every two or three years, luxury life as State Guests, when they visit other States, bungalows rent free, and *amazing 200 litres of petrol* when require only 20 litres or less for professional use. Certainly they are no model for austerity and simplicity but ostentation and the State Advocates from Attorney General downwards are equally lavish with security pomp, right and left, and public expenditure on this score is very high. In short, a human judge and a human attorney are the rarest of the rare, because our sense of development is distorted. Here Gandhiji has observed: *"In so far as we have made the modern materialistic craze our goal", he wrote, "so far are we going downhill in the path of progress".* Legal aid to the poor has many dimensions and all of them are now alien as fundamental to professional life. Access to justice is the cornerstone of fundamental rights. The majority in our country is below the poverty line and the justice system must be tuned to this economic reality. Otherwise, the Constitution is rehetorical illusion and the pledges under it find no fulfilment. Let me hark back to lives of Robert Frost.

The woods are lovely, dark, and deep,
But I have promises to keep,
And miles to go before I sleep,
And miles to go before I sleep.

We, the Senior Advocates of India make a long march and keep the promises. These are the agenda of national development which are materialist and spiritualist and transcend ideological conflicts. The same great ideas hortatively expressed by noble idealist and cyclonic sadhu Swami Vivekananda, is strongly but picturesquely quoted by me in the aforesaid judgment. Swami Vivekananda in a torrent of words exhorted an upper class audience thus:

"Feel, my children, feel for the poor, the ignorant, the downtrodden; feel till the heart stops and the brain reels and you think you will go mad.

"We talk foolishly against material civilization. The grapes are sour... Material civilization, nay even luxury, is necessary to create work for the poor. Bread; I do not believe in a God, who cannot give me bread here, giving me eternal bliss in heaven. Pooh; India is to be raised, the poor are to be fed, education is to be spread, and the evil of priestcraft is to be removed...more bread, more opportunity for everybody.."

Every time I put the question to myself who is a human judge, I am inspired by the noblest and the most glorious thought, expressed by that cultural volcanic wonder who is holistic, hallowed and humanist in the Everest of mighty thought, prompted by heart and head of the highest human beings. I quote that passage, which expressed my view of a human judge, whose functional foundation is a global social philosophy, which brings humanity together :

Let me tell you a few words about one man who actually carried this teaching of Karma-Yogi into practice. That man is Buddha. He is the one man who ever carried this into perfect practice. All the prophets in the world, except Buddha, had external motives to move them to unselfish action. The prophets of the world, with this single exception, may be divided into two sets, earth, and the other holding that they are only the messengers from God; and both draw their impetus for working from outside, however highly spiritual maybe the language they use. But Buddha is the only prophet who said, "I do not care to know your various theories about God. What is the use of discussing all the subtle doctrines about the soul? Do good and be good. And this will take you to freedom and to whatever truth there is". He was, in the conduct of his life, absolutely without personal motives; and what man worked more than he? Show me in history one character who has soared so high above all. The whole human race has produced but one such character, such high philosophy, such wide sympathy. This great philosopher, preaching the highest philosophy, yet had the deepest sympathy for the lowest animals, and never put forth any claims for himself. He is the ideal Karma Yogi, acting entirely without motive, and the history of humanity shows him to have been the greatest man ever born; beyond compare; the greatest combination of heart and brian, that ever existed; the greatest soul power that has ever been manifested. He is the first great reformer the world has seen. He was the first who dared to say, "Believe not because some old manuscripts are produced, believe not because it is your national belief, because you have been made to believe it from your childhood; but reason it all out, and after you have analysed it, then, if you find that it will do good to one and all, believe it, live up to it, and help others to live up to it". He works best who works without any motive, neither for money, nor for fame, nor for anything else; and when a man can do that, he will be a Buddha, and out of him will come the power to work in such a manner as will transform the world. This man represents the very highest ideal of Karma-Yogi.

Our watchword will be acceptance and not exclusion. Not only toleration, but acceptance. Toleration means that I think that you are wrong and I am just allowing you to live. I believe in acceptance. I accept all religions that were in the past and worship them all. I worship God with every one of them, in whatever form they worship Him. I shall go to the mosque of the Mohammedan; I shall enter the Christian's church and kneel before the crucifix; I shall take refuge in a Buddhist temple, where I shall take refuge in Buddha and his law. I shall go into the forest and sit down in meditation with the Hindu, who is trying to see the light which enlightens the heart of everyone.

> *Not only shall I do all these but I shall keep my heart open for all that may come in the future. Is God book finished? Or is it still a continuous revelation going on? It is a marvelous book - these spiritual revelations of the world, the Bible, the Vedas, the Koran and all other sacred books – are but so many pages, and an infinite number of pages remain yet to be unfolded. I would leave it open for all of them. We stand in the present, but open ourselves to the infinite future. We take in all that has been in the past, enjoy the light of the present and open every single window of the heart for all that will come in the future. Salutation to all the prophets of the past, to all the great ones of the present, and to all that are to come in the future.*

In this global hospitality of culture, we discover a glimpse of who is a human judge conceptually and semantically impregnated with profound feeling of humanity and empathy. This I consider, is the heart of a human judge integrated into our system. Parsis, Christian and Muslims and so all religions are part and parcel of our global cyclopedia of our culture. In this rare moral holistic unity, we abolished divisive religious thinking and obdurate obscurantism.

This is a happy blend of justice social, economic and political which, is quintessential conscience of our Constitution. Prof. Griffith in his book 'The Politics of the Judiciary' has cited Winston Churchill and Lord Scrutton to throw light on impartial judges sans class-bias which I repeat here:

> *"The courts hold justly a high, and I think, unequalled pre-eminence in the respect of the world in criminal cases, and in civil cases between man and man, no doubt, they deserve and command the respect and admiration of all classes of the community, but where class issues are involved, it is impossible to pretend that the courts command the same degree of general confidence. On the contrary, they do not, and a very large number of our population have been led to the opinion that they are, unconsciously, no doubt, biassed."* (Winston Churchill : The Politics of Judiciary, *p. 173)*

> *"Where are your impartial Judges? They all move in the same circle as the employers, and they are all educated and nursed in the same ideas as the employers. How can a labour man or a trade unionist get impartial justice? It is very difficult sometimes to be sure that you have put yourself into a thoroughly impartial position between two disputants, one to your class and one not of your class."*
>
> (Lord Scrutton : *The Politics of the Judiciary,* p. 173)

Undoubtedly, impartiality and integrity, accountability to the larger community and transparency in the glasnost dimension of the judicial process are invaluable attributes of a human judge. Usually, we assume these virtues in their Lordships, as writ in the black robes, but often, even law lords have shown the result to be vulnerable on this score. For instance, an outstanding Q.C. like D.N. Pritt has observed :

D.N. Pritt in his autobiography told of his many political cases and of one which 'came before a judge of a great experience and knowledge, so bitterly opposed to anything left-wing, that he could scarcely have given a fair trial if he had tried'.

Are such phrases applicable today? Every practicing barrister knows, before which judges he would prefer not to appear in a political case because he believes, and his colleagues at the bar believe, that certain judges are much more likely than others to be biased against certain groups, like demonstrators or students or certain kinds of action, like occupations of property by trade unionists or the homeless.

This however is to say little more than that, as we have already remarked, judges are human with human prejudices. And that some are more human than others. (*The Politics of the Judiciary,* p. 30/31)

Prof. Griffith in his book 'The Politics of the Judiciary' has quoted from the famous judge Lord Haldane which is revealing in this context :

"I fought my hardest for the Dutch prisoners before the Privy Council this morning, but the tribunal was hoplessly divided and the anti-Boers prevailed over

the pro-Boers. It is bad that so much bias should be shown but it is, I suppose, inevitable."

Even the great Lord Denning was prejudiced towards coloured jurist and later apologized for it. Judges have vast powers to decree huge compensation. It is often said that justice must be fair and seems to be so often times, as Frankfurter had pointed out:

"Judges as persons, or courts as institutions, are entitled to go greater immunity from criticism than other persons or institutions. Just because the holders of judicial office are identified with the interests of justice, they may forget their common human frailties and fallibilities."

In these circumstances it becomes necessary to scrutinize antecedents of a judge and his other social factors, before being sure of his neutrality. That is why an Appointment Commission should be formed. Competent persons of a high level of public credibility and high sense of morality, should be members of the Commission and should be accessible to employers and employees, socialists and capitalists, minorities and majorities, pro-Government and anti-Government - a class-free perspective. Difficult to secure in our days of polemical politics and everyone, which has his own predilections and the process of selection must be transparent, the public being taken into confidence with due publicity.

Secrecy in the process of selection is the upas tree under whose shade reason fails and justice dies. As is proverbial: 'Caesar's wife must be above suspicion'. So must be our judges to command the great trust which gives them the status to criticize the highest executive and even the proceedings of the legislature.

Statutory guidelines and due publicity process must be prescribed for the Preamble, parts III, IV plus IVA must find explicit expression therein, for adoption of selection of judges. Rules of good behaviour unanimously passed at Chief Justice's conference and approved by Supreme Court judges already exist, which can be the basis or criteria for recruitment of members from the bar and subordinate judiciary. The Commission should have an investigation body for plenary powers for getting information about the antecedent, family background and assets and business relations which condition the economic outlook of the judges. The moral, mental, material and spiritual dimensions and background of the judges to be selected, must also be laid down by Parliament. More than all, it is my view that like in the USA, a Rajya Sabha judicial sub-committee must interview critically the candidates for the higher judiciary and thoroughly examine the antecedents from top to bottom without inhibitions and their approval will be the last decisive voice. True, this will make the candidate getting through the rarest of the rare in a society like ours, with feudal, colonial and theological divisive infirmities. The critical episode makes delinquent judges like a camel and the eye of a needle. Strict procedure may be required to get the right candidate on the Bench. Candidate so selected, not on the basis of communalism and other oblique criteria but on merit, is the special function of the Appointment Commission to undertake a sophisticated job.

The candidate so selected should also be efficient and up to date with the due developments of jurisprudence like environment and ecology and other developmental trends of modern technology with impact on social justice and biosphere and revolutionary changes in the economy of the country. Here begins the performance of the judge where arrogance, arbitrariness, class-bias will operate. This means, a compulsory course of six months in the college for judges must be obligatory and a constant review of the judgments must be under scrutiny of juristic bodies. Here comes the importance of a Performance Commission which even David Pannick QC has suggested for Britain. Why not India too?

What is impartiality vis-a-judge? He has to be learned in the glory of India's struggle for swaraj, the history of humanity and secularist semantics from Jesus, Vedic Thought which begins with the first verse of Prophet Muhammad who found an Arab society of havoc, terrorist suppression of women and godist pluralist chaotic pantheon syndrome and transformed it into an orderly humanist cosmos sans chaos and a Bharat Mahan of which Max Muller researched and discovered. Real politics and patriotism is cultural in its roots. Read Max Muller on Vedic India :

> *"If we were to look over the whole world to find out the country most richly endowed with all the wealth, power, and beauty that nature can bestow - in some parts, a very paradise on earth - I should point to India. If I were asked under what sky the human mind has most fully developed some of its choicest, gifts, has most deeply pondered over the greatest problems of life, and has found solutions of some of them, which well deserve the attention even of those who have studied Plato and Kant – I should point to India. And if I were to ask myself from what*

literature we here in Europe, we who have been nurtured almost exclusively on the thoughts of Greeks and Romans and of one Semitic race, the Jewish, may draw the corrective, which is most wanted in order to make our inner life more perfect, more comprehensive, more universal, in fact more truly human a life, not for this life only, but a transfigured and eternal life – again I should point to India."

A judge should be:

"I venture to believe that it is as important to a judge called upon to pass on a question of constitutional law, to have at least a bowing acquaintance with Acton and Maitland, with Thucydides, Gibbon and Carlyle, with Homer, Dante, Shakespeare and Milton, with Machiavelli, Montaigne and Rabelais, with Plato, Bacon, Hume and Kant, as with the books which have been specifically written on the subject. For, in such matters everything turns upon the spirit, in which he approaches the questions before him. The words he must construe are empty vessels into which he can pour nearly anything he will. Men do not gather figs of thistles, nor supply institutions from judges whose outlook is limited by parish or class. They must be aware that there are before them more than verbal problems; more than final solutions cast in generalizations of universal applicability. They must be aware of the changing social tensions in every society, which make it an organism; which demand new schemata of adaptation; which will disrupt it, if rigidly confined." **Learned Hand**

The forensic culture of Kerala, of Gandhi as a paradigmatic judge in South Africa, of Maveli as a legendary ruler of Kerala and his jurisprudence, silhouetted in Volume-I of the Law Reforms Commission, Kerala and be proud of those values in public and private life. Such is a human judge who will be his brother's keeper who will be remembered long after he has gone as one who is never tuned to grab power or gain publicity, or satisfy his pride or prejudice. My humble homage to a Human Judge is in this perspective. The Supreme Court, on my retirement, gave me a touching send off, a delectable dinner and most moving resolution of appreciation as follows:

> *"Permit us to remind you that the Bar is the judge of judges and no judge can avoid or escape the verdict of the Bar. We have summoned you this evening to hear our unanimous declaratory verdict. Our verdict is a decree of affection and admiration. Let us also declare, in these proceedings which are sui generic, that we are not only your judges but also your judgment-debtors.*
>
> *"No words of prosaic prose would be adequate to encompass your vitality and versatility – not even if we drew upon and borrowed from the hoarded wealth of a vast vocabulary you are known to possess. We shall therefore crave your indulgence to supplement the record by those profounder feelings, which the language of the lexicon cannot communicate and which are best conveyed by the language of the heart.*
>
> *"It was in stormy weather that you first book your seat on the Supreme Court Bench on 17th of July,*

1973. Some members of the Bar were apprehensive that your appointment may not contribute to the traditions of judicial detachment. But those who came to scoff, stayed on to respect and to admire. Last Thursday the weather was crisp and bright. But in the Court where you sat, there was a humid air. Eyes were moist. We felt that a great intellectual and a great gentleman was sitting in the Court for the last time.

"In a span of a little over seven years, you have brought distinction to the highest Court of the land. Indeed you did more than that. You opened its doors wider: to the poor, the needy and the indigent. Your crusade for legal aid and law reform, you concern for and commitment to the common people, your dedication to the creed of human rights, and your allegiance to judicial independence and Rule of Law have become quintessential catalysts in our legal process. These humane contributions have endeared you to one and all and will long be cherished and remembered in and out of law reports and in and out of law courts.

"Yours has been a restless and rebellious quest for justice. You have dared and defied and you have drawn your sword of thoughts and words when many would have been content to be reticent and complacent. Your ideas have seldom failed to stir and to provoke. Sometimes you may have gone too far and sometimes you may not have gone far enough, but at all time, there was unfailing courtesy and consideration going hand in hand with a spiritual translucence and equipoise of goodwill, sincerity, compassion and understanding in your

judicial and extra-judicial pathways. All that we will remember and cherish for a long-time.

"There are many landmark judgments you have handed down which have helped to humanize our legal system, particularly in the field of criminal jurisprudence and jail reforms, and which have helped to resolve critical intricacies of constitutional law, harmonizing its delicate equations, optimizing fundamental rights and extending the frontiers of the accountability of the State and its instrumentalities in their ever-expanding operations. Many of your judgments have given a new dimension and a new direction to law. In many of them, you rode the unruly horse of public policy with exceptional skill, acumen and erudition and brought it to heel on the path of justice and good conscience. In some of them you rode it too hard. But there was always your shining faith in the true role and destiny of law in a developing society, which made you the lyricist, the poet-laureate and the visionary of a socially aware and socially accountable Third World jurisprudence.

"We honour you with all our hearts and we bid farewell to you with our warmest good wishes and with our most affectionate homage of respect and admiration."

Address was read out and presented by Dr. L.M. Singhvi, Chairman, on behalf of Members of the Bar, Assembled at Phoolwari Banquet Hall, Pragati Maidan, New Delhi on Saturday, the 15th November, 1980.

The Capital Foundation Society, Delhi wrote to the Chief Minister of Kerala pleading for a National Chair:

Appeal to The Hon'ble Chief Minister of Kerala

Dear Sir,

Greetings. It is a matter of great honour that our founder Patron Justice V.R. Krishna Iyer is the most respected judge this country has produced. His judgments are cited throughout the globe by jurists and human rights champions.

There is no other judge in the world on whom so many students have done research and have been awarded Ph.D., conferred doctorates. In the year 2009 itself, he was awarded a Doctorate by the Chancellor His Excellency M.C. Bhandare of the Utkal University.

Justice Iyer was conferred the Highest Russian Honour by President Putin at New Delhi. He received the biggest reception and highest Award from President Najibullah at Kabul. It was my privilege that on both the occasions I was present. He is one of those patriots who has never shirked responsibility, and has expressed freely whatever is in the interest of vast millions. He transcends all political parties and speaks fearlessly what he thinks right.

You know his contribution to Kerala more than any one else, as he had been a Minister in EMS Government, a Judge of Kerala High Court, Chairperson of several social and cultural organizations and finally for his radical Legal Reforms Committee Recommendations.

We have issued an appeal to many people to persuade you to institute a Chair in most Kerala universities known as Justice V.R. Krishna Iyer Chair and a National Chair in the newly created Central University in Kerala.

With kind regards,

Yours sincerely,

Sd/-

Dr. Vinod Sethi

This flattering function does not glorify me into a human judge. One swallow does not make a summer. Let me cite what I have written in my book *Off the Bench:*

Moderation is a fatal thing; nothing succeeds like excess - wrote Oscar Wilde, good for literary lampoon, not for forensic praxis. And yet, the elation of elevation to the high Bench seduces some robed brethren to imitate simian fashion, the Oscar dictum; and in this 'excess' process, intemperately indulge in pejorative denunciation of brethren of the lesser judiciary and thereby caricature the judicature. In our country, while other constitutional functionaries forfeit their credibility by ludicrous circuses and corrupt delinquency, the judicial fraternity, by and large, has preserved its dignity, decorum and sobriety, although exceptions, deviances and heady hubris abound, born of the illusion of occupying the commanding heights of constitutional authority. British judges on the Bench have, in the past, been boisterous and buffooning but have vastly improved. The awe of the court hall and the moderation of judicial diction are a paradigm. David Pannick, in his book judges writes :

"Mr. Justice Jackson of the US Supreme Court observed in 1952 that 'men who make their way to the Bench sometimes exhibit vanity, irascibility, narrowness, arrogance and other weaknesses to

which human flesh is heir'. It would be surprising, indeed alarming, if some of the eminent legal minds that constitute the English judiciary did not, on their rare off days, act injudiciously. This was recently recognized by Lord Chancellor Hailsham. Those who sit in judgment occasionally become subject to what he called 'judges' disease, that is to say a condition of which the symptoms may be pomposity, irritability, talkativeness, proneness to obiter dicta (that is, statements not necessary for the decision in the case), a tendency to take short-cuts. A 'judge may grow unfit for his office in many ways'."

In our country, judicial aberration, linguistic indiscretion, irritating observations and violent diction, slowly escalating, have produced a demand for canons of judicial conduct.

A robed umpire, exercising authority with modesty and refusing to be authoritarian by issuing ukases, and admonishing lesser tribunals using unbecoming expressions of abuse is the desideratum. A code of conduct for judges is very much being debated and Justice Verma, when occupying the Chief Justice's position took the initiative and got a code drafted and approved by the higher judiciary unanimously. A public demand for a judicial performance commission, comprehensively overseeing appointments, behaviour, transfers and censure when needed, by appropriate constitutional amendment, is now a public issue. Some aggressive judges, some corrupt tribunals, some immoderate, intemperate and uncivil judicial personnel mar and tar the otherwise excellent reputation of the robed class. They forget that the Bench is no immunity when vices abound and criticism cannot be silenced if good behaviour, ethics and gentleness are jettisoned seeking refuge in judge power and contempt power.

Is this credential enough to claim title as a Human Judge? Perhaps the Central Government without much research nor getting my consent bestowed on me the human distinction of Padmavibhushan among few judges. The Executive is not the best judge of judges. Still it is of some value. I was in Delhi when the Collector of Kochi telephoned me asking for my consent for this honour. I first declined since I was in Delhi and desired to know the grounds on which this honour was bestowed on one who was a critic of many State policies. I asked Rashtrapathi Narayanan himself, the highest Executive: Sir, I am a critic of your Government although I am an admirer of Jawaharlal Nehru for his humanism. Of course, not all the Nehrus deserve adultation. President Narayanan was a liberal soul and told me: Sir, you must accept it. Your criticism is always motivated by a constructive correctional humanist purpose as the last letter of Nehru to you testifies.

(Circuit House)

Dehradun

May 24, 1964

Dear Krishna Iyer,

Your letter of the 15th May reached Delhi when I was away in Bombay for the A.I.C.C. meeting. Hence the delay in answering it.

I am glad you have sent me an account of the Budapest meeting of International Democratic Lawyers. I agree with you that these meetings should not be wholly ignored, and I hope that our External Affairs Ministry will pay attention to them in future.

Yours sincerely,

Sd/-

Jawaharlal Nehru

Shri V.R. Krishna Iyer
Advocate
M.G. Road, Ernakulam

There is no malignancy about it. Democracy requires a critical public opinion. Even after receiving the distinction you are free to criticize my Government from a human, cultural angle. Therefore he persuaded me and I consented to be Padmavibhushan which I received the next day from him. The great Justice Gajendragadkar had received it. He was a Human Judge under whom I was a beloved member. Truly Dr. Narayanan was a liberal democrat, Harold Laski's good student and head of an eminent educational institution namely Delhi University.

I remembered my days as SPCA Secretary from my days in Tellicherry. Later, when I was minister I made the Kerala Government pay the salary of SPCA Inspectors of the state, the only State in India, and when I was Secretary I myself visited slaughter houses and prevented cruelty in killing of cattle. Later, I became Vice President of the Animal Welfare Board at the request of Rugmini Devi of Adayar. My links with animal welfare are strong. But is that a component of a Human Judge. Perhaps, yes, because I remembered *51A* which speaks of humanity and also *'compassion for all living creatures'*. I also recollected a philosophical definition of God. God sleeps in the mineral, wakes up in the vegetables, walks in the animal and thinks in man. Darwin has proved that the human is an evolution from animals and still retains many savage qualities of beasts:

> *We must, however, acknowledge, as it seems to me, that man with all his noble qualities...still bears in his bodily frame the indelible stamp of his lowly origin.* **(Darwin)**

So I felt that to love animals is to be human and to be savage is to be cruel to living creatures.

Then I remembered by strong allergy against death sentence. All Life is dear and God-given. Mahatma is a sublime humanist and against Capital Penalty; Macaulay was great as a penologist, not a humanist. In *Ediga Annamma's case (1974 4 SCC 443) and Rajendra Prasad's case* (1979 3 SCC 646) I held, contrary to conventional judicial thinking shaped by Macaulay's criminology, a humane sentencing policy against death sentence conditioned by Mahatma Gandhi which *de facto* abolished capital penalty based on humane considerations. Chief Justice Ray was apparently told that I had nullified death sentence and sent for me to discuss this unconstitutionality of my penology during lunch interval. I met him. Brother, have you declared death sentence *ultra vires*? You can't do that because a Constitution Bench has already upheld death sentence. With some embarrassment, I explained to him, assuming death sentence constitutional, the option for the court to lay down guidelines as to when it should not be imposed and the life term was appropriate. He agreed with hesitation my explanation. However, some of my sadist colleagues did not cherish my weakness against death penalty and in a later case held before a larger Bench that, it should be imposed *only* in cases of the rarest of the rare instances. This is neither Macaulay nor Mahatma who was against death sentence altogether. Later, I was invited by Amnesty International aware of my conviction against death penalty, to inaugurate an International Conference at Stockholm against death sentence along with Swedish Prime Minister which I did. Of course, the government of India declined to pay my travel at their expenses. But the Amnesty did meet my expenses. I stand for a Reformation theory of sentencing jurisprudence even to the extent of suggesting that transcendental meditation is therapeutic sentencing strategy. Will this make me a Humane Judge? The great Lord Scarman once wrote to me a private letter dated 6th October 1982 that he was moved by my passion for life in *Ediga Annamma and Rajendra Prasad* and chose to follow it in his judgment in a Privy Council ruling. Here is the letter:

> "Dear Judge,
>
> *I am sending you a copy of the Privy Council Appeal judgment from Jamaica. The case is Riley v. The Attorney-General. You will see that Lord Brightman and myself in our dissenting opinion made very great use of some observations of yours in the Indian Supreme Court.*
>
> *Thank you so much for the really passionate way in which you have in the past and continue now to forward the cause of human rights."*
>
> Yours sincerely,
>
> Sd/- Scarman

Scarman is not an Indian judge but a celebrated British Law Lord. Of course, Britain has abolished death penalty by law. God gives life and He alone can take it is the Gandhian view. But savage barbarity is terrorist ubiquity, over the globe today. How can this be obviated?

I wonder whether the Senior Advocates of India have considered these factors while calling me a 'Human Judge'. Their verdict is Indian Bar wisdom.

Access to social justice is a structural basics of our Constitution and so I claim that *Law India* must preserve its cultural glory in the spirit of Max Muller or Mahatma Gandhi or Nehru or Dr. Ambedkar. Every judge should be a human judge - Not the deterrent committed to the Reformatory theory nor retributive theory of sentencing.

I pay my great tribute to the Senior Advocates Association of India for being Indian. Once this cultural fundamental becomes quintessential to our judicial jurisprudence there will be a transformation of our jails as I did make Kerala jails, a hospitable rehabilitation home. Every criminal is born innocent and has a finer future that is the kernel of the *Valmiki Jurisprudence.* Valmiki, who was a robber, became a Rishi by a saintly mantra. Our paramount duty is to be truly socialist, secular and democratic Indian. Our patriotism, our felicitous fellowship glory of all true religions, which in Vivekananda's words, are a manifestation of the divinity in every man.

An honest God is the noblest work of man **(Robert G. Ingersoll).**

Humanism is not merely a sentiment but its roots are green in the heart of man. A bright brain with a hard heart, is a dangerous tool of justiceship. So, a great judge is one with a large heart, not with a sharp brain. That is why our Constitution speaks of sympathy to the lowliest sector of society and special provision for establishing the reality of material and moral equality in life. Indeed, reservation is not discrimination but equalization as a process towards equality. That is why, classless social fabric of socialist society can be harmonized, only with an egalitarian methodology, aimed at providing a level playing field in public life for the high and the humble. Economic equality for the working class, justice is the due labour jurisprudence. I am for this dynamic economic justice, not for working class greed, grab and indiscipline in hartal. If we take justice, social and economic seriously, a new perspective towards the working class and industrial relations will be necessary, as I have explained in Gujarat Steel Tube's case. A fair deal to workers make them contended in the industry and the management told me years later, that the workers produced more after a just wages in the Gujarat judgment and the management secured more profit from the Industry. I have founded a new liberal jurisprudence for women producing domestic justice and family welfare. I have expounded this thesis in the report of a Committee of which, I was the Chairman appointed by Margaret Alva to look into the injustices suffered by women in custody and to suggest remedial measures. My report was motivated by compassion for sisters. Narasimha Rao promised publicly, he would implement but did not. Likewise, our children are neglected and exploited and became street children and adult goondas. The State of India did not care to implement an International Convention on the rights of a child though a signatory to it. Because of his long indifference and culture of torture of children, the UNICEF appointed a committee with me as Chairman to implement this Convention for the rehabilitation of victims of pediatric exploitation. My Report was received by the then Prime Minister Vajpayee with praise but not yet implemented, is proof of the callous attitude of Executive and Parliament of the State. These remakrs have some bearing on my post retiral, *free* activism of a *human judge*. Forgive me for this autobiographical adventure.

The largest minority under economic disablement, is the considerable humanity below the poverty line, largely belonging to the agricultural dalit sector. That is why suicide cases escalate in the rural sector. Extremism and terrorism, which go together, increase in our villages and one way of overcoming misfortunes and indebtedness is abolition of alcohol and drug addiction and agricultural development, which finds an easy Western market in our agrarian backwardness. Therefore, the elimination of poverty and unemployment have many social blessings, including domestic contentment, child development and care. Abolition of privation of human rights, gender justice and the evils of alcoholism is absolutely necessary, if the disasters, consequent on liberalization of alcoholism, are not arrested totally. The Law Reforms Commission has quoted a judgment by the Chairman in the Supreme Court, in Volume I of the Report at page 165, advocating moderation because of the outrageous impact of alcoholism on social and domestic peace, stability, security and public health of society. It violates a directive principle of state policy, which de facto demands abolition. It is a curse that several State Governments in succession are making and encouraging use of beverages sales as a source of revenue. The only State Government, which believes in respect for the Constitution on this core, is the Modi Government in Gujarat, where the Chief Minster told me that, it was 60 to 70% successful as an abolitionist State. On the other hand, in Kerala licenses for bars and clubs and restaurants are increased and every toddy shop has long queues and no dry days at all. One Collector who banned it, was duly transferred. Every festival, whatever the religion, is now an invitation for drinking. Yet not any molecular or molar party, even during election season, has the sanity to ask for prohibition, despite a strong judgment of the Supreme Court and increased violence in street fighting, terrorism, domestic discord, ragging, immoral abuses of girls and ubiquity of psychotropic drugs. Behind every evil of this type, is the alcohol. By advocacy of prohibition, its recognition in the humanity will stop. Today, although I know some colleagues robed (robed brethren) drink privately and some dare though rare, sit tipsy on the Bench!

Access to justice is through litigation in our adversary system. Litigation costs being heavy and lengthy and horrendously dilatory, is the distance between the beginning of a case and its finality of the *lis*. So much so, the great Learned Hand cynically remarked that every litigant before he goes to court must execute a will, as to who will continue the case after his death, since man lives in the short run but litigation never dies and lives in the long run. The multi-decked hierarchy of courts, makes it a baffling astrology as to when to predict finality or binding infallibility. There is no endeavour to streamline litigative life or legal aid to the poor on a realistic basis.

Way back in 1957 when I became a minister for Law in Kerala, I had prepared a comprehensive legal aid scheme the like of which no other State had. The all India Law Minister's Conference of 1957 September (?) lauded this scheme as a model but it died with my departure from the ministry. No State Government, even my successors, are bothered about the indigents although I made some beneficial provisions in the Court Fees Act, providing no court fee for claims of wages of workers and maintenance for widows. Had it been implemented early, more could have been done through the legal *benefit fund,* which I had provided in the Court Fee Act. But the poor man's cause is nobody's concern, not even in left feudal colonial State. The People's Council for Social Justice (PCSJ) was established by me and the Ford Foundation was pleased to make a substantial grant for running it. Its first glorious annual meeting was a grand adventure in Paravur (North) with the whole district participating at the *people's level* and many disputes got settled on the spot. It was inaugurated by Chief Justice Chandrachud and if similar experiments continued, this nation would have been a happy sanctuary for legal aid. Similarly, when I was member of the Central Law Commission, I was appointed by Indira Gandhi as Chairman to make a report on free legal services to the indigent. A comprehensive report was made by me. Only fragments of which are implemented. Why? The poor man will not win election? But communalism will win. So, a vote bank, not the constitution is politically in operation. Let the people judge. Through election campaigns, the ballots can be bought by slogans, and processions propaganda and not by the indigent slum and homeless humanism. The constitution is dead, so too Gandhi. Narasimha Rao reversed Nehru who has become irrelevant. America is dominent. What a fall my countrymen! The Human Judge sans ideological oxygen will suffer suffocation.

Public Interest Litigation and Access to Justice

Many common issues affecting the communities will come to the court on an individual basis, if he has a personal grievance, personal cause of action, since the British jurisprudence reorganizes only individual standing. This narrow concept of cause of action is contrary to socialism, social justice and democracy in its collective dimension. To democratize and collectivise judicial access, is what is in Ratlam Municipalities case. (AIR 1980 SC 1622). Where cause of action or standing is not confined to the individual injured but needs broadening the scope of legal remedies. It occurred to me that this narrow conception of standing was anti-socialist and lucky in the Ratlam Municipality case. I expanded the jural semantics of standing and access to justice. This gives rise to Public Interest Litigation. In a poor country like ours, Public Interest Litigation is fundamental ideology of *Poverty Jurisprudence* and is now integral to *Law India.* Any one, not an official busybody with private motivation, but social concern and public spirited activism, can come to the court, urging a common cause affecting public wail and interest. He can even write letters to the court, which will make a preliminary investigation and if satisfied that there is the voice of public grievance, take up the matter and hear and decide. Of course, the affected party will be heard. This is the democracy on judicial remedies with epistolary procedural jurisdiction. It has worked well and deserves to be statutorised with fair restriction to forbid abuse of this process.

I claim as a mere matter of history that I gave shape to PIL and Justice Bhagvathi ably reinforced it. This perhaps is a useful dimension of a human judge. Those allergic to PIL have no socialist conscience or desire for justice to have-not humanity.

The well-being of society through forensic process must justly extend even to law making. To humanise, socialise and secularise the rule of law, is basic to our tryst with destiny. This is exemplified by the Law Reforms Commission, Kerala, for which, the Kerala State forced Chairmanship on me. I am old and ill but the Law Minister gave me no option. As Chairman of Law Reforms Commission, Kerala, with the assistance of a few colleagues, the following Bills, among 104 of them we have proposed, were recommended, which strengthen the socialist, secular and democratic character of the State and ministers. They are :

1. The Kerala Police Act.
2. The Kerala Widows' Right to (a shelter and maintenance Bill .
3. The Kerala Rights of illegitimate children.
4. The Kerala Code for Custodial, Correctional and Habilitating Justice to Women Bill.
5. Right to a small farm and shelter Bill

6. The Kerala women's Code Bill
7. The Kerala Access to Justice Bill.

The motivations for these reforms are, human rights of the common man. Am I a human judge for this reason? I wonder. The legislative objectives were promotive of human rights, right to life and equality and dignity in society.

My basic points about a human judge are over but a recondite search into my past, at what learned lawyers of high standing to name me as a human judge; made me discover a few more remote points, which I set out below. Not a boast but facts, which I blush to mention.

If I am humane and gentle on the Bench and kindly to living creatures, I must frankly shift the tribute to my kindly mother, who lived as an obedient wife of my father. He was gentle and lenient but was stern as a father and husband. Home is the best school and mother, the finest teacher. So, it is that, I owe everything good in me to my mother who was always kind to the poor and gave food to hungry persons, who came to our home and got hospitable food; never for once was harsh to the have-nots, but was so loving and sweet as the breast milk she gave me. The happiest moment of my life of course, was her warm lap. Truth to tell, was Sarada's luscious laps, while in long car journeys to Coorg for cases, which were a shade sweater. A judge would be human only if his domestic felicity was real. Yes, I had a fine conjugal home and this made my life loving on and off the bench. Work hard without being tired since her presence was perennial healer. It is from this spring of piety, the heart of this source of goodness and cosmic devotion that I possess and practiced kindness. I have seen at the Bar, the same compassion from lawyers happy at home but bitter and irritable of conjugally quarrelsome. The Bar was my teacher of law in the same spirit Holmes has stated it: "Shall I ask what a court would be, unaided? The law is made by the Bar, even more than by the Bench". In this background, read my expressions on the Bar and the Bench and social justice and forgive me if I am exaggerated or being harsh. Read every judgment or brief order, my sympathy will be testified by it. I have reversed myself on the same point of law that counsel has changed my mind by more fruitful arguments. Law is what judges say. It is but what judges write, which is persuasively presented by charming submissions of counsel. Presentation is advocacy. Of course, police torture have hurt my heart in me. That is why, I abolished hand-cuffing, solitary confinement and any trace of torture in prisoners. My judgment in Nandini Sapthathi case a few other judgments and my post-retiral articles, you may pick anyone. You will notice a sense of humanity. Maybe, it is a weakness or goodness but there it is. Call me human judge or weak judge. But that is the judge I was for what it is worth. Read on and judge me at the end.

In an article *from Macaulay to Mahatma* in my book: *Law, Lawyers and Justice,* which I presented some years ago; its few passages may be relevant. I quote them: "This culture of humanism, compassion and habilitation, this faith in personhood and its great potential, that seeks expression but suffers suppression in an unjust social system, consists in the trinity of principles of Karuna, Samata and Praghna which the Buddha taught. For this Gandhi fought. It is the value-oriented jurisprudence, *where man matters* more than money. Its springs are globally found in the progressive affirmation by the United Nations Charter of 'faith in the Magna Carta and fundamental human rights, in the dignity and worth of the human person, in the equal rights of men and women'. What a universal heritage with a dynamic, *satvic dimension* in penological perestroika Humanism in criminology, or satvalogy, if I may call it so, is having a hard time. Therefore, compassion towards those who indulge in savage crimes under drives of passion, fights on with *faith in Man* in the manifestation of the divinity in Man. Bernard Shaw once remarked: "All great truths begin as blasphemies". Valmiki was a violent robber until he was transformed by a mantra Ram, Ram to become the world's greatest poet.

My last thought which is also the first thought about a human judge is that *he* is a human judge for whom *Man Matters* more than materialist pleasures. Our cultural collapse has begun the day we made our journey downhill and money mattered and hunger of Third World was Big Business for the corporate consumerist cosmos. To reverse this perverse trend, is the object of social justice where man matters above all (vide my judgment in Sunil Batra reported in AIR 1978 SC 1675 and Maru Ram reported in AIR 1980 SC 2147). In Churchill's words humanism is better than legalism. My such conviction is a proof of my concern for prisoner's reform and my connection against death sentence.

In the beginning is the end. Who is the Human Judge? He who answers Socrates:

> *Over 2,000 years ago, he says, Socrates said, "Four things belong to a judge; to hear courteously, to answer wisely, to consider soberly and to decide*

impartially.' At NJC we honor that and also strive to improve a judge's competence, conduct and productivity." (Quote It-I, p. 201)

In Learned Hand's erudite prescription:

'May I take an illustration nearer to the field with which you are especially concerned? I venture to believe that it is as important to a judge called upon to pass on a question of constitutional law, to have at least a bowing acquaintance with Acton and Maitland and Gandhiji as a successful lawyer in South Africa, with Thucydides, Gibbon and Carlyle, with Machiavelli, Montaigne and Rabelais, with Plato, Bacon, Hue and Kant, as with the books which have been specifically written on the subject. For in such matters everything turns upon the spirit in which he approaches the questions before him. The words he must construe are empty vessels into which he can pour nearly anything he will. Men do not gather figs of thistles, nor supply institutions from judges whose outlook is limited by parish or class. They must be aware that there are before them more than verbal problems; more than final solutions cast in generalizations of universal applicability. They must be aware of the changing social tensions in every society which make it an organism; which demand new schemata of adaptation; which will disrupt it, if rigidly confined.' (Quote It-II, p. 203)

A truly human judge is one who in my Republic Day Greetings I have described as 'I am a human: I count nothing pertaining to humans alien to me.'

The reservoir of a Bar, is the source from which, selection has to be made to the Bench. The robed brethren before elevation and empowerment in the right to punish with death penalty and huge sum by way of compensation, will have to be tested by their performance as lawyers. It is the best lawyer who can be classified as a good judge but the lawyer itself belongs to a higher professional class. The architect of the rule of law and one who is independent and fearless and fights for justice and truth, earns a finer position in society. The finest tribute to the profession of law is articulated by Felix Frankfurter :

> *No one can be a truly competent lawyer unless he is a cultivated man. If I were you, I would forget all about any technical preparation for the law. The best way to prepare for the law is come to the study of the law as a well-read person. Thus alone, can one acquire the capacity to use the English language on paper and in speech and with the habits of clear thinking, which only a truly liberal education can give. No less important for a lawyer is the cultivation of the imaginative faculties by reading poetry, seeing great paintings, in the original or in easily available reproductions, and listening to great music. Stock your mind with a deposit of much good reading and widen and deepen your feelings by experiencing vicariously as much as possible, the wonderful mysteries of the universe, and forget all about your future career.*

Similarly the high aristocracy of this learned profession can be gathered from what Abraham Lincoln himself said:

> *There is a vague popular belief that lawyers are necessarily dishonest. ... Let no young man choosing*

the law for a calling for a moment yield to the popular belief - resolve to be honest at all events; and if in your own judgment you cannot be an honest lawyer, resolve to be honest without being a lawyer. Choose some other occupation, rather than one in the choosing of which you do, in advance, consent to be a knave.

I have been influenced while on the Bench and on the Bar by what Alexis Tocqueville has observed:

In America, there are no nobles or literary men and the people are apt to mistrust the wealthy; lawyers consequently form the highest political class and the most cultivated portion of society... If I were asked where I place the American aristocracy, I should reply without hesitation that it is not among the rich, who are united by no common tie but that it occupies the judicial bench and the bar.

Having said what I regard as the finer qualities of the Bar, I would assert that the best lawyer is eligible to shine as a human judge. I do not think that this species is extinct. The point is, we have to create a social milieu for the profession to give great recognition not by the income he makes but by the integrity he manifests. For Indians the best paradigm of a lawyer is Mahatma Gandhi.

Some Trans-Atlantic Tremendous Trifles of recondite relevance to my humanism

My son Ramesh Krishnaiyer was an engineer under Johnson and Johnson Controls in Milwaukee, the business capital of Illinois, the land of Lincoln. I used to visit that city frequently. Over the collective leftist elements of Lincoln's Illinois, the politicians gave me a reception. There was a decent gathering. I was surprised. In many local policies there was more socialist slant in the USA than in India. I spoke first and emphasized not the arms deal dollar grants and the Nuke Treaty as a gift from the White House and World Bank aimed at making our colonial foreign policy a dependencia syndrome. A sound Sterling empire gone and dollar domination gained. But I stressed that Gandhiji, our spiritual guide was a disciple of Thoreau who observed: 'Under a government, which imprisons any unjustly, the true place for a just man is also a prison' and how Martin Luther King was in turn, Gandhiji's disciple? How Vivekananda became famous after his great Chicago speech and J. Krishnamoorthy and other great Indian gurus had been welcomed with cultural hospitably in USA. Read the Autobiography of Mahatma Gandhi. In the higher sphere of human thought, we had bright bonds, forgot the nuclear deal and arms terrorism and Big Business MNCs of America Inc. What amazed me most was the American Presiding gentleman's one-minute speech when I finished the value-wonder bond between our two great nations. He simply stood up and said that this great talk of Mr. Iyer made me feel my blunder in not bringing my tape recorder to record this great address, brief but brilliant. The USA is not mere materialism but has a basic cultural hospitality. Do you know that a few miles from Harvard, Swami Vivekananda was holding Yoga classes with success?

Again Maharshi Mahesh Yogi has two Universities teaching Vedanta in Ohio and Washington but none in India. The West learns from hallowed East. But the East goes downhill from the consumerist West.

Yet again, I was struck by the marvelous popularity of Mukthananda with orderly crowds listening to his discussions anywhere from New York to California. I have attended his discussions to large American audiences. So also the Brahmakumari movement. Read the epic poet of Vedanta Walt Whitman and lofty thinkers.

These are the lasting ties between the soul of the USA - not dollarmania of commercial five-star culture.

Emerson and Walt Whitman were finest advaita in their thoughts more than the spurious godmen of Bharat. I was once invited to address in Stanford Varsity on Legal Aid in Asia. I spoke for an hour on Asian Poverty and the need for the Jurisprudence of Penury and Public Interest Litigation. John Kennedy's brother-in-law, Sargent Shriver presided. I spoke of the divinity in the lowliest and the legal value of egalite in the Supreme Court social philosophy, which shall not be the conscience-keeper of the capitalist class and the princes. An hour long performance and a silent audience. Shriver, at the end of it, got up to wind up with one sentence. How I wish I had a Justice Krishna Iyer in the Washington marble Judicial Palace! Such in brief are some of my experiments with truth, which have a bearing on my career as a judge. The most sensational of my judgments for which Seervai, my great critical jurist paid me a tribute, is the conditional stay of Indira Gandhi's disqualification as Prime Minister. That mystic judgment has made many wonder as a piece of enigma but I claim every part of the judgment which produced friends and foes for me, is truly my experiments with truth. Did this independent pronouncement persuade the senior advocates regard me as a Human Judge? Ultimately what is truth is as difficult a question as asking *who am I* or *know thyself.*

Aham Brahmasmi! This profound issue takes us to the social philosophy of justice and truth. The nidus of the judges is the Bar and therefore the Gandhian perspective of the legal profession becomes relevant while dealing with the Human Judge as a higher category of the judicial profession.

'Gandhi as a Jurist'

I have no doubt that when the sponsors of today's symposium chose the subject of Gandhiji as a Jurist, they did not have in mind the term jurist in its ordinary technical sense. But I do not think that we shall be doing any injustice to Gandhiji's memory, if we do not describe him as a jurist in that sense. It cannot, however, be denied that Gandhiji had a legal philosophy of his own and entertained most refreshing views as to the duties and functions of lawyers as well as of courts of law, though they might not have gained acceptance in those days and might not get even today, a wholehearted acceptance. That, however, cannot detract from their value and the fruitfulness of a discussion, like that of today's evening.

Gandhiji's views regarding the duties and functions of the legal profession must find the first mention in any discussion of his legal philosophy. According to him, though a lawyer must do his very best for his client, he ought not do so to identify himself with his client, as to transgress the principles of truth and justice ...

Gandhiji always regarded that over and above, the interests of his clients, he had a prior and perpetual retainer on behalf of truth and justice. That led to his developing certain rules of conduct which he scrupulously followed.

His adherence to justice and truth also led to another result. Gandhiji was always in favour of settling a case and often advised his clients not to fight to the bitter end. That is illustrated by the very first case in which, he was concerned on behalf of his employer one Abdulla Seth, between whom and the opponent Tyeb Seth, he was able to bring about an amicable settlement. This practice often creates a misconception in the clients' mind, especially in the case of junior lawyers. But in Gandhiji's case, it brought him greater esteem and confidence on the part of his clients. To clients who were co-workers in his public work in South Africa, Gandhiji had always stressed that it is the glory of the legal profession to bring the two opposing parties together, to agree to submitting their disputes to arbitration.

One final point I have done. A reference cannot be avoided to Gandhiji's views on civil resistance, which is an important part of his legal philosophy. Some of you might remember, how strongly he protested against the dictum of the Bombay High Court that "those who live by the law, must keep the law". Commenting on this Gandhiji wrote:

"If it means that no lawyer may ever commit a civil breach, without incurring the displeasure of the court, it means utter stagnation. Lawyers are persons, most able to appreciate the dangers of bad legislation and it must be with them, a sacred duty by committing a civil breach to prevent a criminal breach. Lawyers should be guardians of law and liberty and as such, are interested in keeping the statute book of the country 'pure and undefiled'."

It is perhaps true, that a situation contemplated by

Gandhiji may not arise in an Independent India, with a Constitution based on democratic principles. But when a body of lawyers condemns in strong terms, legislative measures of Government as unconstitutional and objectionable, as has happened in recent times and may happen in future, it would be an interesting speculation as to what Gandhiji's reaction would have been, if he had been alive today and shared the views of these lawyers.

As all of you are aware, Gandhiji was considerably influenced by the teaching and writings of Ruskin, especially his Unto The Last. This is what Ruskin wrote on the function of the five honourable professions, to be found in any civilized society.

"Five great intellectual professions relating to daily necessities of life have hitherto been in existence - these exist necessarily in every civilized nation; the soldier's profession to defend it; the pastor's to teach it; the physician's to keep it in health; the lawyer's to enforce justice in it; the merchant's to provide for it. And the duty of all these men is, on due occasions, to die for it. On due occasions, namely the soldier, rather than to leave his post in battle, the physician rather than to leave his post in plague, the pastor rather than to teach falsehood, the lawyer rather than countenance injustice. What is the due occasion for the merchant? It is the main question for the merchant as for all of us. For truly, the man who does not know when to die, does not know how to live." (From the speech delivered by late Mr. Justice B.N. Gokhale added as Appendix III to the Book "The Law and the Lawyers" by M.K. Gandhi).

OMEGA

Law, Lawyers and Judges

The human judge is a rare product in Indian jurists society, because he is conditioned by his class milieu which moulds his moral and material faculties. Why? Because all creation developmentally responds to environment. Society gives the Bar a monopoly because the right to life in dignity and wellbeing depends on the extent to which the rule of law governs the value of life. He lives in a community where the rich rule the social institutions and its trinity of Montesquieuan instrumentalities in a democratic Republic. The poor man matters little even during election because his ballot is bought and sold by the highest bidder who belongs to the richest party or is himself very wealthy. In short, democracy can be manipulated by the affluent wing of the mafia sector. The best constitution fails to inhibit operation of the *robber class* with the result that the rule of law is functional as a rule of robbers. Here is the need of the human judge for whom justice, socialism, economics and politics are parts of his professional integrity and non-negotiable mindset. The lawyer by principled professional values, gives sound advice and can arrest malpractices and clean up society and social transactions. Indeed more than any other profession, the lawyer is the architect of the finer fabric of social structure. So far as India is concerned, we have viable value-based Constitution which should be the foundation, the vision, the mission and even the passion and conviction of professional conduct. Our Preamble makes our Republic socialist, secular and democratic. These three expressions must be seen as a sublime semantic. So much so, every national policy, election manifesto and legislative bill, if contrary to these values must be struck down by the judiciary to be ultravires. The judges, therefore, must have a social philosophy, consistent and vibrantly supporting the Constitution whose conscience is compassionate to the have-not humanity and the weaker sections of society, and the comity of plural religions and the divinity and dignity of every member of humanity. Backwardness of women is to be vanished and ensured. No theological pathology can contradict the Socialist Secular Democracy of our Republic. No canon or command from outside can survive so long as the Constitution is sovereign and supreme. Indigent and backward children must have free and compulsory education at State expense. Development and public health and communal comity and social welfare must be under State care, rich or poor, and is secular and no Pathri or prophet or acharya can infringe secular policy. A crime free society, non-violence, truthful and animal non-sacrifice and abolition of casteism is a fundamental value and should be guaranteed in the larger community. The basic moral principle, whatever the religion must govern theology and anything contra, is anti-secular and unconstitutional. Basic equality, economic and social, is integral to socialism. Theology has no immunity from immorality in the larger sense, as the constitutional semantic obligatory. The rule of law must protect these values of the suprema lex.

Take care of the moral stature of the Bar and the unity and integrity of the nation and the sublimity and humanity of the Bench will take care of itself. Every judge comes from the Bar and the humanity of the lawyer, once inviolable, ensures the humanist integrity of the judiciary. The lawyer interprets the Constitution and the Bench is bound by the Constitution. So too the policeman and the Executive in all its ramifications. If the legislature and the Executive act unconstitutionally, the court has the power to nullify its action. Every citizen has a discretion to disobey any action of the State if it is plainly unconstitutional as the Supreme Court has ruled it (AIR 1974 (SC) 147). Unfortunately, our Central Executive contravenes constitutional basics but our politicians hardly make these fundamental flaws, part of the political electoral polemics.

To sum up Who is a Human Judge, I have nothing more to say as my memory at this old age cannot dig up state anecdotage. After all my dotage now relies on the cyclonic Sadhu, my eloquent inspirer, a cultural wonder. And my forensic wonder is M.K. Gandhi whom I quote. He is my last word on a Human advocate. 'Listen: The Shavian remark to Gandhiji's son on his assassination, is a warning to every great glorious martyr in every profession. It is dangerous to be too good.' (Bernard Shaw)

Arbitral Alternative of Litigative Disputes

One of the scandalous features of our forensic system is the intolerable delay of litigation, longest in the world affecting public interest and the poorer section of the people. The litigation relating to the land dispute connected with the Babri Masjid is nearly half a century old. Had it been decided within half that time, the question of Babri Masjid and the shocking communal terrorism would never have occurred? Thus, it is a very urgent policy to shorten litigation by alternative dispute resolution process. One of them is reducing the number of appeals and revisions. But Parliament in its creative sloth has not chosen to explore this possibility. Another common place alternative is arbitration for which we have an Arbitration Act. The pivotal methodology is undertaken judicially by retired judges. It is true that the arbitration is essentially judicial and the appropriate cadres to operate it functionally is judges. One should have welcomed it on a large scale but alas the retired judges are hungry to make arbitration a remedy which aggravates the melody defeating the blessings of litigation by making the whole process extravagantly expensive and longer in all the vices of the curial litigation. Easy adjournments, huge remuneration and the whole device a racket and mafia - vicious. Judges when they retire make in a few hearings of arbitration cases, what they in their whole career have not made as judges. A sense of discipline fee regulation, suitable to the moderation time vice and promptitude and other good behaviour is necessary by procedural behavioural code for arbitration judges with a performance commission which would be empowered to give directions to arbitration courts. A panel for selection is also desirable. These will turn up arbitration as a healthy alternative, which will also cast an obligation to conciliate and settle disputes with judicial powers. I suggest a comprehensive code for arbitration on the lines indicated above.

I must confess that my experience of post-retiral arbitration, because of my conviction that judges should not be capricious or avaricious in running after arbitration and collecting unconscionable sums of money, which makes the judicial institutions as money-making commercial operation, forfeiting the confidence of the people in the economic sobriety of judicial officers. These abuses, which are now rampant, must be restrained by the code. Arbitration should find its finest hour by conciliation and dispute resolution by consensus. In this connection, the only arbitration where both sides approached me together and wanted me to be an arbitrator, I settled avoiding cantankerous finale but a happy harmonious settlement. The concluding paragraphs of that benign adventure, are set down below for its educational value:

> *Justice has an aspect of relativity; and what all disputants, on fair and competent advise, accept as just, is the best that human institutions can dispense. I have always regarded that the finest hour for the Bar and the Bench arrives when a long drawn-out and extremely bitter litigation has been brought to a peaceful end, by mild suggestions from the Bench, catalytic action by advocates and sensible response from the parties. I record my deep appreciation on the counsel, appearing for the various parties in the present case, for having produced what, I am assured by counsel, is a reasonable and just solution, wrought in a spirit of peace and goodwill. Justice is what justice does.*

To be a judge is a model life; abstemious, not five-star transparent public and private life, nothing sweet or suspicious. But showing power, class-conscious costly perks, high salaries and elite company and even alcoholic dinners, flags flying on cars, pompous security as VIP as if office proclaims the man. Is not the Bench recruited from the Bar? Must first simplify the Bar before preaching to the Bench. Correct. The fabulous fees of senior advocates humbles every other profession except the corrupt politician and bureaucrat and the PWD, which Rajaji described as public enemy number one. Rightly, a severe ceiling on lawyer's fees is basic, if right to justice is fundamental. The legal system is currently hard currency and balloon remuneration. So, making the Constitution is a caricature in the adversary system; where the sophisticated methodology keeps the have-not majority alien, untouchable and unapproachable unless his purse is fat and liberal. So, the Bar Council must obligate a sharp, penological provision against this pathological syndrome and comprehensive legal and poverty jurisprudence. This is the first and before a judge's moral code. The life of the law is not logic but experience and so the rule of law must reflect the rule of life. The structural architect of Social Justice is the legal profession simplify, streamline and transform it to be an instrumentality of a poor people, sans caste, creed, minority and majority. This is the desideratum of Law Reform of swaraj in its vision, mission and passion.

To praise a human judge on the higher bench of judges of India when the women representation is negligible, is to ignore gender justice and half of humanity. So, it is for the better that a human judge needs as a condition precedent a descent representation of women on the Bench. I take pride in saying that the first woman judge in India, Anna Chandy was elevated under pressure from me as Home Minister, way back in 1958. Alas, even today the percentage of women is grossly under-represented. Such things first.

Social justice is a fetch where gender justice is a facet. So I appeal to the Indian Association of Sr. Advocates to demand to the Central Government to give their sisters a fair share on the Bench. No civilized State can command the rule of justice without giving this structural basis, constitutional expression as a priority.

To expect a generation of human judges when the nidus namely Indian Bar is not elevated to the highest standards with the sublime constitutional values, tuned to social justice, economic justice and political justice of democratic Republic is bathetic and pathetic. Therefore, a generation of human advocates is a condition, precedent to the basic question of 'Who is a Human Judge'. First thing first.

While I speak of a human judge or a human advocate, cynicism is impossible to eliminate and the world's most sarcastic figure, I have not come across, is a Hallowed Human Judge currently crucified on the multi-national corporation cross by the contemporary judicial incarnation of Pontius Pilate, who crucified innocent Christ in a barbarous sentence. The justice system is today a travesty and social syndrome as Bernard Shaw in characteristic sarcasm has expressed in acid ink, in acid print :

> *He who has never hoped can never despair.*
>
> *The one point on which all women are in furious secret rebellion against the existing law is the saddling of the right to a child with the obligation to become the servant of a man.*
>
> *The greatest of evils and the worst of crimes is poverty.*
>
> *Money is Almighty save on Sunday inside Church.*

> *Our political experiment of democracy, the last refuge of cheap misgovernment.*
>
> *Democracy substitutes election by the incompetent many for appointment by the corrupt few.*
>
> *There is nothing so bad or so good that you will not find Englishmen doing it; but you will never find an Englishman in the wrong. He does everything on principle. He fights you on patriotic principles; he robs you on business principles; he enslaves you on imperial principles. He rules Indian colonial Cabinet.*

An Indian who obeys the command of the American White House is like an Englishmen who does evil on principle. He can be human even in Third World conditions (and India with its huge majority below the poverty line is one) without the State being structurally democratic. Poverty is Big Business for U.S. MNCs travesty unless economic democracy which is socialist secular and have-not humanity, has a dominating voice over fundamental State Policy, geared to Swaraj values, never to bend before imperial MNC Big Business or theological pathology submitting to God and Godmen as Big Business. 'A Supreme Divinity or honest God is the noblest work of man'. (Ingersoll) Egaliterianism and humanity in both materialist and spiritual dimensions is the revolutionary version of the basic structure of our Republic and the Human Judge must use his powers to make this a rule of law and rule of life or else the constitutional transformation is a myth, a majestic illusion, a robe of robbery. The Human Judge must have this social philosophy. That is the Judiciary's Tryst with Indian human Destiny. Sans this, Truth and Justice proves a puppetry of democracy as satiriced by the anonymous sardonic poem :

The law locks up both man and woman
Who steals the goose from off the common,
But lets the greater felon loose
Who steals the common from the goose.

The life of a Human Judge is more decidedly, the highest of robed brethren. Homer is not more decidedly the first of heroic poets. Shakespeare is not more decidedly the first of dramatists. Demosthenes is not more decidedly the first of orators and Boswell is the first of biographers than the Human Judge, the finest symbol of Social Justice in our Socialist Secular Democratic Republic. Who he is; will be history's verdict! Not I, please. This I say in spite of the great jurist Seervai's glorious comment on my judgment in Prime Minister Indira Gandhi's case refusing Palkhiwala's plea for an absolute stay of the Allahabad High Court's order, unseating Indira Gandhi from her Prime Minster's position.

Why I say no please? Burke gives the answer :

Magnanimity in politics is not seldom the truest wisdom; and a great empire and little minds go ill together.

The glorious judicial empire and small robed brethren hardly go together. How can I claim to be a builder of India's constitutional judicature? Even so, let me cite Seervai in partial extenuation of the label Human Judge applied to me:

As the historian turns from the High Courts to the Supreme Courts, his task will be harder, for the history of the Supreme Court during the emergency is a history of two different periods: the first began a day before the Emergency and ended with Prime Minister Indira Gandhi's Appeal in the Election case; the second began with the Habeas Corpus Case and ended with the revocation of the Emergency by a defeated Mrs. Gandhi, unwilling to put into the hands of her opponents, a weapon she had forged and used against them. Of the first period, the historian will say that the Supreme Court moved towards its finest hour, a day before the proclamation of Emergency, when, on 24 June 75, Krishna Iyer J., following judicial precedents, rejected an application made by Mrs. Gandhi that the Allahabad High Court's order, finding her guilty of corrupt election practices and disqualifying her for 6 years, should be totally suspended. In the best traditions of the judiciary, Krishna Iyer J. granted a conditional stay of the Order under appeal, although he had been reminded by her eminent counsel, Mr. N.A. Palkhivala, "that the nation was solidly behind (her) as Prime Minster" and that "there were momentous consequences, disastrous to the country, if anything less than the total suspension of the order under appeal were made."

In reinforcement of the above thought, there is Sri. Fali Nariman's testimony in a long ago article of 2001 in *The Hindu* which runs:

Eighty-seven still batting!

Mr. V.R. Krishna Iyer's most outstanding contribution has been that whatever he has given to the law, he has also given unstintedly to public life. He has given unstimtedly to public life. He has exhibited that inestimable quality – so rare these days – of his public pronouncements always coinciding with his private opinions.

An assessment of Mr. Krishna Iyer's contribution to the law by reference to his prolific judgments – more than 700 delivered during the seven years that he sat on the Bench of the country's highest court – would not do him adequate justice. It would only help collate a wide range of flamboyantly-phrased judicial opinions on a variety of subjects. I believe his contribution to Indian jurisprudence is much greater. Justice Krishna Iyer, more than any other Judge by his pronouncements on the Bench has made other Judges think! Through his judgments, he showed to them (and us lawyers) that the Anglo-Saxon system of jurisprudence India had adopted (and adapted) did work, if only we knew how to make it work: which was to decide (as one must), according to law, but never to forget that law without justice, is like an egg without its yolk, and much of its salt!

He was responsible for – and in turn inspired – a new thrust, a new direction, for decision-making in the Supreme Court. He helped to humanize the legal system – particularly in the field of criminal jurisprudence and jail reform.

He extended the frontiers of the accountability of the State and its instrumentalities in their ever-expanding operations. He often strayed from the beaten path of the law, spinning his own cocoon of jurisprudence, making no secret of the fact that a judge must have a social philosophy and a humane approach to legal problems.

Law to him was 'value-loaded'. His social philosophy was more than an interpretative tool. It has been the mainspring of almost all his judicial dicta. He founded a new 'school of jurisprudence' – which had at one time many adherents; now alas, very few.

And then, he had that abiding quality of a great judge – he was fearless. Whilst still a junior puisne judge in the Supreme Courts, within two years of his elevation from the Law Commission to the highest court, he sat as the Vacation Judge during the summer recess of 1975.

It was destined to be the most historic summer recess of the court. Indira Gandhi had lost the election petition filed against her by Raj Narain in the High Court of Allahabad. The High Court judge ruled that she had forfeited her seat in the Lok Sabha. Indira Gandhi applied for an absolute stay of the judgment and order. The matter was argued before Krishna Iyer – the Vacation Judge.

He could have passed the buck – granting an absolute stay till the reopening of the court when a Bench of three or five judges would have finally heard the application. But he did not flinch. Sitting singly and so taking the entire odium on himself, he passed an order granting only a limited stay, consistent with the practice of the Supreme Court in all election appeals.

He ordered that whilst Indira Gandhi as Prime Minister could speak in either House of Parliament (so long as she filled that office) she as a Member of Parliament could not vote nor participate in proceedings of the Lok Sabha – since she had been unseated by the judgment of a competent election court.

India's constitutional expert Mr. H.M. Seervai (otherwise critical of Justice Krishna Iyer and many of his judgments) applauded. In his book on the Constitutional Law of India, he described the passing of the order granting a conditional stay as the "Supreme Court's finest hour."

Great praise, indeed. But then Mr. Krishna Iyer always did what he thought was right – not bothering about the consequences.

His pronouncements when on the Bench and off it (after retirement), have been invariably swadeshi – of an indigenous socialistic bent. But his fame has spread far beyond the country's frontiers. Only a few weeks ago, when I was in Paris attending a plenary session of the International Court of Arbitration of the ICC, an old time colleague on the court, Mr. Antis A. Triantafyllides, a distinguished lawyer from Cyprus, said to me that he had read the Constitution Bench judgment in Fatehchand vs. *State of Maharashtra (delivered in January 1977) and was greatly impressed by the high quality of its thought-content and language.*

I was quite amazed. I asked him how he came to know about it, and he said that he was looking for judgments of courts around the world on debt-relief laws and found that Mr. Krishna Iyer's judgment in Fatehchand case, was the finest. I am privileged to have been (at least in part) responsible for this decision, since I argued the case for the petitioners – and lost!

What has endeared him to us all is that, after retirement he has been a vocal public figure.

He advises no one but public causes, he holds no briefs but for his country. Whenever he speaks on matters of moment, India listens. At eighty-seven he is not old – because, to paraphrase the great poet: 'He shall grow not old as we, that are left grow old. Age shall not weary him nor the years contend. At the going down of the sun and in morning. We shall (always) remember him."

Never in the field of litigative conflict, has so much owed by so many for delivery of justice, civil, criminal and miscellaneous to so few robed brethren, described as human judges, who are free from fear or favour, affection or illwill, as the rarest of the rare, among the vast army of judicial numbers in the uncertain gamble of tier upon tier, procrastinating interminably the final end of forensic justice as in the Indian justice system. I salute this micro-category of daring human judges whose survival is the only hope of those have-not humanities who are now in despair of gaining justice, social, economic, political and egalitarian.

In today's world of flagrant violation of social, economic, egalitarian justice with a value distortion of Money *higher than Man*, a transformation of the Social Order is the desperate desideratum. Homer is not more decidedly the first of heroic poets, Shakespeare is not more decidedly the first of dramatists, Demosthenes is not more decidedly the first of orators, than Boswell is the first of biographers. Human Judge is more decidedly the finest of the Indian Judiciary in fulfilment of the pledge of swaraj, the tryst with Bharat's destiny this century and the Socialist Secular Democratic Republic under the Sovereign Constitution - Not any myopic theological pathology nor nationalist divisive religious breach of the unity, integrity and fraternity of Bharat Mahan.

8

A Crucial Arbitration Case

The case of North East Hill University (NEHU) versus M/s Raj Rewal and Kuldip Singh Architects, was referred to me for Arbitration by Guwahati High Court in 1988. After perusing all the relevant records, I proceeded to hear the case in detail and gave the Award, which satisfied both the parties, having litigated for 11 years.

The Supreme Court has preferred pragmatism to principle, swiftness to soundness and declared that the jurisprudence of arbitration may jettison *rationalization* in awards. Within the law, order may be brief but never a blank. At the end of a long *litigious* journey the case ended happily in a mutually agreed adjustment.

With both sides in despair and unable to extricate themselves from the opiate project, many sensitive institution switch from 'robed' **judicialese** to arbitral alternatives. The NEHU had selected Sri Raj Rewal, a renowned architect with trans-national laurels for his performances. His drawings and models were regarded as deserving of being adjudged the finest. In the competitive exercise in excellence, he was given the contract for bringing into being the University building. A formal agreement was executed in 1978. It contained a complex of clauses, with lacunose looseness in places specifying the rights and obligations of both parties so interwoven that breach somewhere could spell breakdown everywhere and to mar the process of smooth progress. What began well in 1978, it did not take long to get bogged down in difficulties; each side blaming the other for defaulting.

In order to get a comprehensive idea of the crucial issues, it was consensually decided that a visit to the Shillong campus was necessary before proceeding in Delhi. Myths and realities were separated with engineering dialectics at the site of the project. Temper of discussion in Shillong swayed the Delhi courtroom with gentle suggestions. The flexible responsiveness of both contenders had a catalytic effect; side stepping preconditions and preconceptions for an early end to the bleeding bout.

The learned counsels on both sides presented reasonable and just solution. Justice is what justice does. After visiting the site I felt sad that a decade has passed and yet the country witnesses only the preliminary edifices. The contract of 1978 ran into rough weather and was replaced by another, signed in 1985 with modified terms, which was terminated by the Vice Chancellor. The matter reached High Court, which referred back to Vice Chancellor for arbitration. He appointed me – retired Judge of Supreme Court – as the Sole Arbitrator on 16 October 1988.

The secretarial staff appointed by me, officers of the NEHU, advisers, counsellors of both parties and the Architects gave commendable input to come to the Agreement. Being involved in highly intricate issues, my job could not be so simplified without their constructive approach. It was left to me to state what the terms of the Award are. The Vice Chancellor and other party wrote me to decide the case without recording further evidence although the evidence had not been completed and arguments not yet addressed. Both sides wrote to me to accept my Award.

The Terms of Award:

> Good sense smiling and sunshine of conciliation precluded any need to argue out my conclusion in this Award. Cancellation of the contract on 21 May 1986 was rescinded to the satisfaction of the Architects. University had to rectify the defects noticed during the inspection by me and the architect-assessor.

Both sides agreed to have no more rights against each other. Merits of the case were not mentioned in the direction for payment. The claimant was to be paid a sum of Rs. 28 lakh in two equal instalments on 31 March and 31 May 1990. Late payment was subjected to interest of 12 per cent. Both litigants were kept away from the cost.

Award was pronounced on 23rd November 1989. Both side agreed to share the payment of Arbitrator and associated staff. Both parties were free to select and take their records from the Secretaries within a month. Unclaimed records were to be disposed of by the Secretary.

9

Election Commissions : Matter of National Public Debate

(*a*) The Constitution contemplates a free and fair election and vests comprehensive responsibilities of superintendence, direction and control of the conduct of election in the Election Commission. This responsibility may cover powers, duties and functions of many sorts, administrative or other, depending on the circumstances.

(*b*) Two limitations at least are laid on its plenary character in the exercise thereof. Firstly, when Parliament or any State Legislature has made valid law relating to or in connection with elections, the Commission, shall act in conformity with, not in violation of, such provisions but where such law is silent, Article 324 is a reservoir of power to act for the avowed purpose of, not divorced from, pushing forward a free and fair election with expedition.

Even so, both Articles 327 and 328 are 'subject to the provisions' of the Constitution which include Article 324 and Article 329. Since the conduct of all elections to the various legislative bodies and to the offices of the President and the Vice-President is vested under Article 324(1) in the Election Commission, the framers of the Constitution took care to leaving scope for exercise of residuary power by the Commission, in its own right, as a creature of the Constitution, in the infinite variety of situations that may emerge from time to time in such a large democracy as ours. Every contingency could not be foreseen, or anticipated with precision. That is why there is no hedging in Article 324. The Commission may be required to cope with some situation which may not be provided for in the enacted laws and the rules. That seems to be the raison d'etre for the opening clause in Articles 327 and 328 which leaves the exercise of powers under Article 324 operative and effective when it is reasonably called for in a vacuous area.

"Once the appointment is made by the President, the Election Commission remains insulated from extraneous influences, and that cannot be achieved unless it has an amplitude of powers in the conduct of elections – of course in accordance with the existing laws. But where these are absent, and yet a situation has to be tackled, the Chief Election Commissioner has not to fold his hands and pray to God for divine inspiration to enable him to exercise his functions and to perform his duties or to look to any external authority for the grant of powers to deal with the situation. He must lawfully exercise his power independently, in all matters relating to the conduct of elections, and see that the election process is completed properly, in a free and fair manner.

An express statutory grant of power of the imposition of a definite duty carries with it by implication, in the absence of a limitation, authority to employ all the means that are usually employed and that are necessary to the exercise of the power or the performance of the duty.

———

The Commission is, therefore, entitled to exercise certain powers under Article 324 itself, on its own right, in an area not covered by the Acts and the Rules."

The Election Commission is thus not only entitled to take all steps, but is under a constitutional obligation to do so, in order to maintain during elections, communal harmony, which is a necessary condition for holding free and fair elections according to the Constitution.

It may not only direct political parties not to field a particular candidate who vitiates the atmosphere but also direct any person making a communal speech that seeks to polarise voters, not to make any speeches during the election process. And if any such person violates the code of conduct, it may even direct State governments to detain such a person in custody during the period of the elections.

The Election Commission would understand the width and amplitude of its vast powers under Article 324 and exercise them pro-actively for the conduct of elections in a proper manner.

10

Governor: The Only Constitutional Ceremonial Head of a State

India fought for long years for Swaraj, led by the Indian National Congress and Gandhiji. He too was eliminated when an Independent India became free from the supremacy of the crown and Rajen Babu became the President as declared by the Constitution of India. The freedom of India under the Independence of India Act, was passed by the House of Commons, overruling Winston Churchill's Opposition which ran as follows: "Power will go to the hands of rascals, rogues and freebooters. All Indian leaders will be of low caliber and men of straw. They will have sweet tongues and silly hearts. They will fight among themselves for power and India will be lost in political squabbles". The Viceroy represented the Queen in his relation with the native princess and was Governor General in his dealings with the Governors of the State. Both these offices ceased to exist when the Constitution replaced them. When all the princedoms integrated into the Republic, the supreme head of the country was designated the President of the Constitution.

Was he a prophet? The Congress Party asserts that the Governor, a nominee of the Congress in power at the Centre with benami or dubious authorization, has discretion to disobey the Cabinet ruling in the State.

Wide and limitless power is dictatorship by the backdoor, stultifying the democracy of the Constitution. Is this Nehru's Congress?

Our constitutional basic structure is democratic and non-negotiable. When after the debacle, consequent on China's invasion the Congress demanded of Nehru the dismissal of Krishna Menon, and Nehru disinclined. He had ultimately to yield since, that is the democratic imperative, not leaving a discretionary decision to the party President. The Congress in Kerala is innocent and illiterate of political and judicial precedents and judicial case-law on the point in India or England. The Supreme Court has made the law clear in Shamsher Singh's case by a seven judge Bench. As Home Minister, I forced Governor Rao to accept my decision for commutation whether he liked it or not. Why the NDF or LDF are so ignorant and aggressive against the Advocate General, though the issue is so critical in the corrupt, confusing, political situation?

Seven judges bench in Shamsher Singh's case, has finally laid down the law that the Indian administrative system is substantially based on the Westminster system where the queen is bound to follow the Cabinet's advice except in a few rare exceptions illustratively mentioned not exhaustive. Though, in that ruling, such as where the Cabinet decision is irrational or arbitrary or perverse or plainly blatantly biased or malafide, the Governor may have a discretion but the rule which democracy implies is that the Governor is the ceremonial head but the real power of administration is with the Council of Ministers. To assume, as the opposition in Kerala desiderates, that the Governor has a free indiscriminate discretion to substitute his judgment for that of the Cabinet, is a grave outrage from the basic structure. Otherwise, the Governor may assume all executive power, refuse to sign legislation passed by the legislature and negative judicial decisions. Thus, our Constitution will be reduced to a paper tyranny. The implication of the Governor being treated as vested with absolute power, is dangerous. Imagine the Rashtrapathi acting as the sole ruler not accountable to anyone except his conscience. Swaraj becomes a mirage and absurd. The Cabinet system of Government as against the presidential system, virtually makes the monarch or the President a figure-head, because sovereignty is in the hands of the people represented by their elected deputies who in the last analysis constitute the Cabinet. Royalty was rejected but the ideology of the crown haunted our constituent assembly that is how the Rashtrapathi and Governor survived verbally. The office of the viceroy survived in the shape of a Governor General and ended up in the shape of presidential symbol. But to go back from the President to a symbolic crown representative with totalitarian powers is absurd. Rare exceptions are necessary in the political compulsions of certain situations. That is how, in Shamsher Singh's case the court after a lengthy discussion ruled, that the President was bound by the Cabinet decisions and asked the question: Is the President a cipher? No, a few exceptional situations may still demand the independent judgment of the Rashtrapathi. The list cannot be exhaustive, as in the case of age of the judges when there is a controversy. Even there, the President has to consult the Chief

Justice of India and has to act on his advice, not as he pleases. That is how, Chief Justice Raghavan became a casualty.

Once we have accepted a Cabinet system of Westminster tradition, it is full of guidelines including even removal by threat of impeachment Vide Edward the VIII. The fact remains that Shamsher Singh's case (of seven judges) until reversed by a larger bench or by radical change in the Constitution, without violating the basic structure, will still govern the Governors and the President. I know of no case of the Supreme Court, which dissents from Shamsher Singh. The Madhya Pradesh ruling, propagandised by the Congress Opposition in Kerala, is an egregious folly. Every later case has affirmed Shamsher Singh and provided one or two additional restricted exceptions in consonance with the earlier case. A passage or paragraph from the Madhya Pradesh ruling of the Supreme Court of five judges confirm my contention:

> *A Division Bench of the Bombay High Court dismissed the Revision Application, but whilst dismissing the application it was recorded by Gadgil, J. as follows:*
>
> *"However, I may observe at this juncture itself that at one stage it was expressly submitted by the learned counsel on behalf of the respondents that in case if it is felt that bias is well apparently inherent in the proposed action of the concerned Ministry, then in such a case situation notwithstanding, the other Ministers not being joined in the arena of the prospective accused, it would be a justified ground for the Governor to act on his own, independently*

and without any reference to any Ministry, to decide that question."

In short, unless the present Kerala enigma is so irrational, or grossly contrary to precedents, it is not proper or legal for the Governor to depart from the rule that the Cabinet decision binds Rajbhavan. Why embarrass the Governor for gaining political power by polls, where the final word belongs to the ballot of the last man. Churchill put it powerfully: 'At the bottom of all tributes paid to democracy, is the little man, walking into a little booth, with a little pencil, making a little cross on a little bit of paper - no amount of rhetoric or voluminous discussion, can possibly diminish the overwhelming importance of the point'. No.10 Downing Street, prevails over Buckingham Palace.

Our founding fathers in their wisdom, were familiar with the British practice symbolized by the Thames. In constitutional law, Westminster was our model, not Washington and the presidential system. To adopt a passage from Shamsher Singh:

Prime Minister Nehru explained the position with political clarity when moving the clause relating to the election of the President:

'One thing we have to decide at the very beginning is what should be the kind of governmental structure, whether it is one system, where there is ministerial responsibility or whether it is the Presidential system as prevails in the United States of America; many members possibly at first sight might object to this indirect election and may prefer an election by adult suffrage. We have given anxious thought to this matter and we came to the very

definite conclusion that it would not be desirable, first because we want to emphasize the ministerial character of the government, that power really resided in the Ministry and in the Legislature and not in the President as such. At the same time, we did not want to make the President just a mere figurehead like the French President. We did not give him any real power but we have made his position one of great authority and dignity. You will notice from this Draft Constitution, that he is also to be Commander-in-Chief of the Defence Forces just as the American President is. Now therefore, if we had an election by adult franchise and yet did not give him any real powers, it might become slightly anomalous and there might be just extraordinary expense of time and energy and money without any adequate result.'

It follows that the Cabinet binds the President and the present case unless an exceptional situation has arisen or the Cabinet decision is irrational, manifestly biased or intentionally calculated, to save a constitutional authority, the rule that the tenant of the Rajbhavan, is bound by the Cabinet ruling and the Governor cannot substitute his separate judgment or of any jurists, who may be his favourites, to impotentize the Cabinet's clear resolution.

True, the CBI has suggested that Pinaray Vijayan, Party Secretary is guilty and should be prosecuted. But on matters of law, it is not the police chief but the highest law officer of government, whose advice the Government must follow in propriety. In the present case, the Advocate General has exonerated Pinaray Vijayan and the Government is, unless there is some manifest bias for the Advocate General in favour of the party secretary, propriety requires the Cabinet to adopt his advice. The opposition may request the Advocate General to appear before the House and seek clarification which is a dignified way of Nehru's party, instead of burning his effigy or abuse him. Has politics become lunatic for the sake of power? No. Commons or Crown; people's representatives or authoritarian Rashtrapathi, who governs Bharat Mahan!

11

Bureaucratic Instrument - A Splendour or Syndrome

The finest hour of administrative felicity dawns when a collective bureaucracy, committed to the values of the Constitution and concerned to carry out socio-economic justice to have-not humanity, heartily and creatively promotes the quintessence of democracy and access to rights and reliefs in dynamic fulfilment.

A bureaucrat is a brave builder but this desirable species is a rare wonder. A peculated Bureaucrat is a ruler by paper power, not popular and therefore a common disaster. Bureaucracy has become a universal phenomenon, believe it or not, representing a pragmatic organ of every government and public institution, irremovably operating with rigidity and indifferent to vote banks. Any administration which is governed by any political party or front is voted into office by the people, and has its own manifesto. But in actual practice, a paper-logged officialdom controls decisions, unaccountable to the public and pachydermic to noisy criticism. Never-the-less this immobile machine is efficient in its own way and speaks the petrified language of timeless experience. Democracy is

Government, by the people, for the people and responds to popular agitations, communal sentiments, cheap appeals and goes by the sacredness of numbers ignoring the wisdom or critical judgment of cause. Democracy is government by ideology run by the confidence of the majority; bureaucracy is Government by an officialdom with a hierarchical structure, piles of files and routine notings from officer to officer in soul-less sequence and adding little to the merits of the matter. Judges hear both sides and decide by writing speaking judgments. The legislatures hear members, witness vocal battles, shouts and screams and ballyhoos and at the end count votes and pass resolutions by numbers. But bureaucrats, bovine or brisk, sit and rest inside comfortable rooms, visit canteen, read pages, go into committees, meet bosses, examine precedents and inscribe brief conclusions sans arguments and sentiments, busily telephone or receive calls, rarely bend before public opinion and waste time on vocal arguments from both sides but record short sum-ups for ministers to sign 'yes'. Natural justice and case-law citations are not part of their praxis. 'Fileocracy' with notes and signatures of a spiral of officers and the accumulated wisdom of administrative precedents weigh with bureaucrats, not Human Rights, platitudes, democratic movements or political ideologies. Even so, there is much to be said in favour of a government which is run largely by an excellent bureaucracy. Silent perusal of files, constant phone communications, pen-propelled advice or instructions and presentation of perplexing points of view is the role of the clever bureaucracy, the final word, 'yes or no' being formally with the minister. Obliging bureaucrats prepare the paper in tune with 'Yes Minister, No Minister' culture - a pathology when ministers are lay and corrupt. But we need a bureaucracy for precision of decision, awareness of precedents, rules and regulations and principled judgments. Otherwise, the froth of agitations, sound and fury of aerobatic debates in the House, and logomachy of lawyers like in courts will mar administrative orders. Experience, intelligence, imagination and the stored knowledge latent in precedents ensure a certain measure of stability, continuity and reliability so essential in a humanist regime. Absent these features, Administration becomes a functioning anarchy, a chaos in the cosmos, a confusion which unsettles the future, riddles the system and baffles the little Indian. A brilliant, highly learned bureaucracy is an abiding asset and aid to excellence of democracy. A sensitive, people-oriented, academically brilliant and fearlessly truthful bureaucrat is a pillar of good governance. In short, a happy blend of democracy with profound social philosophy and independent, intelligent bureaucracy with flexibility and efficiency, produces a lovely architecture of fine management, political stability and human justice. 'This is a consummation, devoutly to be wished'. This society of darkling politicking and money-making power and corrupt, communal, official crowd, which suffers from the syndrome of unconcern, dilatoriness and cringing behaviour. The patriotic and statesmanly bureaucrat is great figure. The Constitution is a casualty and the Republic, a freebooter's paradise unless a brave, brilliant bureaucracy becomes a Public Service beyond purchase and possesses a sensitive soul ever at the behest of a fine Council of Ministers with integrity who listen, learn and act for the have-not humanity of Bharat Mahan!

12

Lawyers Turn Law Breakers

In our adversarial system in preference to the inquisitorial system, arguments by counsel have a key role to play in discovery of the truth. The Bar, the professional instrument of presentation of cases, is indispensable in the forensic process. As Brandeis observed: *'For a judge rarely performs his functions adequately unless the case before him is adequately presented'*. The great Holmes put it neatly: *'Shall I ask what a court would be, unaided? The law is made by the Bar, even more than by the Bench.'*

It is clear that the best judgment pronounced is the product of the finest submissions at the Bar. In this sense, the lawyer is an officer of the court and is integral to the administration of justice. I hold the view that a good Bar is a great part in justicing and therefore must be given a high place in the fulfilment of the right to justice which is fundamental to all fundamental rights. The Bench without the Bar, is as bankrupt in the delivery of justice as the Bar without an intelligent, impartial, independent Bench to hear and decide. The right to justice is inherent in every citizen; even the devil has that right. It follows that the legal profession has a fundamental morality to present even the devil's case. This does not mean he should falsify to win a case.

The lawyer's dharma as Gandhiji and Abraham Lincoln demonstrated, included a peremptory obligation. Never to refuse brief merely because his case is bad. Gandhiji has said that when a client approached him he would insist of two things. The freedom to tell the court the truth of the case, even if it be against his client. Secondly, a fair compromise, if offered, he should have the authority to accept it without reference to his client. He did both throughout his practice and still enjoyed a lucrative practice and with least loss of income.

The Profession is Noble and those professing it should endeavour to be nobler. However, the same calamitous incidents in the Madras High Court have dealt an indelible blemish to the patrician profession.

Reports suggest that Subramanian Swamy was before the Madurai Bench of the Madras High Court to implead in appending lis and that when he was in court, a few members of the Bar assaulted him in the presence of the judges in the course of his arguments. This is unprofessional and outrageous for any member of the Bar. The police intervened naturally and the focus of the battle shifted. The fight switched over between the lawyers and the police. When violence is committed in public and in court, the policemen in uniform have a moral duty to arrest the assailant be howsoever high. I do not know why the judges did not punish for contempt the guilty lawyers when the contempt was committed in their face. A judge who does not exercise his power when the situation calls for its use, betrays the rob and its authority and thereby brings down the whole judiciary in the esteem of the people. The Bar Council, on his own must initiate action against the delinquent members. Professional morality is a precious asset of the Bar to maintain which is a sine quo non of its sublime status in the scheme of things. The Bar from the Attorney General downwards is not a mere calling for trade or money making adventure. But a noble wing of society, is basically necessary for the rule of law and the democratic Republic itself. The sinners in the profession, knowing the law as they do, are doubly guilty by culpable conduct and unbecoming of their status as officers of the Court in defacing the exalted and rarified pillar of democracy. The lawyers, it is reported behaved barbarian and berserk by setting fire to police stations and motor cars. There is the Goonda Act in Tamil Nadu and the legal profession should be the last to offer offenders and fulfill Churchill who uses the expression rogues and rascals about Indian patriots.

The pity of it, O, the pity of it, is that this arsonist skirmish continued in Chennai City the next day. A judge was hit badly by stone throw. Public vehicles too were set on fire. Police stations were destroyed, public property ignited by obdurate, unregenerate few who persisted in this terrorist incendiary misadventure till the Commissioner of police ordered shoot at sight if anyone was found setting fire to vehicles. He knew his power and the lawyers stopped from their criminal movement. This is bad deviance of the members of the Bar, albeit a miniscule minority, who have held the gallant reputation to ransom. The court is not a private institution and must surely take suitable action. It looked as if the sensitive judges wanted to restore peace and so closed the court for two days. It looks as if the riot police went rampant and beat up innocent lawyers. The criminals as usual have escaped. This incident is a colossal scandal and deserves national concern. The Madras High Court has a great reputation. Now tarnished beyond repair. Belligerency once condoned without deterrent punishment, is apt to repeat itself. The entire judicial system in the country is shaken up. Madras today may be the Supreme Court tomorrow. If justice dies, India's future is a functioning anarchy. Parliament must meet and constitute a national inquiry by a committee of statesmen competent to give, not placebos but paramount prescriptions and proscriptions to the constitutional supremacy. Gandhiji was shot and forgotten, with none to follow him. This time paramountcy is pramountcy and none shall stultify rule of law which shall be the rule of life.

13

Obita Dicta in 15th Lok Sabha Election Petition

This has with reference to the judgment in Bail Application Nos. 539, 1142 and 1209 of 2009 dated 24.3.2009 which contains about today's State Government purely obiter dicta in a simple bail petition which was eventually dismissed.

> *...while unconstitutional exercise of power by the executive and legislative branches of the government is subject to judicial restraint, the only check upon our own exercise of power is our own sense of self-restraint.* (Harlan F. Stone, in *United States v. Butler*, 297 U.S.1, 78-79 (1936).

We are living in a morbid season of election syndrome when every minor social dispute or political scramble is exaggerated out of proportion to the modicum of malady in society. But this is manifestation of executive or political parties, not of the professional judges for whom self-restraint is almost an obligation. Unfortunately publicity is a weakness to which even the old veterans are victims :

> *Publicity is an evil substitute, and the art of publicity is a black art; but it has come to stay, every year adds to its potency and to the finality of its*

> *judgments. The hand that rules the press, the radio, the screen and the far-spread magazine, rules the country; whether we like it or not, we must learn to accept it.* (American Judge Learned Hand)

The Election Commission has warned the politicians not to abuse this sensitive election season to say anything malignant about any party or candidate as it will interfere with the fair poll or just franchise. The judges are above politics and command an attention which other agencies do not have, precisely because of their objectivity, impartiality and political neutrality. Hearing affected parties before they are condemned is a condition, precedent of judicial functionalism. 'Audi alteram partem' is a fundamental of forensic propriety.

> *Audi alteram partem—hear the other side! - a demand made insistently through the centuries, is now a command, spoken with the voice of the Due Process Clause of the Fourteenth Amendment, against state governments, and every branch of them...whenever any individual, however lowly and unfortunate, asserts a legal claim.* (*Felix Frankfurter in Caritativo v. California*, 357 U.S. 549, 558 (1958)

A recent judgment in Bail Applications referred to above from a learned judge of the High Court of Kerala with some executive background who knew clearly the moderation of the judiciary as distinguished from the partisan exaggeration of the executive who, out of political motivation use their prestigious power in their command for election purposes, contains certain bizarre

Obiter dicta, which may have a serious impact on one of the parties involved in the election. This has become so common in many states that a caveat against this anathema is overdue. But for a moment, this basic virtue of political neutrality has suffered an eclipse or oblivion when judges write their diatribes more like an election campaign with bizarre obiter dicta about the law and order situation in Kerala without hearing the State but condemning it. It is an asset for the Congress party and oblique condemnation of the present Government front; both of which are again engaged in a struggle for every seat in the parliamentary election. The case before him - a bail petition needs only a one line sentence or a short statement of facts, but brevity does not win political publicity and so the judge has gone into a galloping hyperbole as if he were campaigning as a candidate denouncing a rival party. Caesar's wife must be above suspicion and obiter dicta are the last refuge of a judge. All that I can say is that a judge, otherwise good in diction and dicta has departed and acted without hearing the State before condemning it:

> *The most satisfactory ideal I have ever been able to form of justice is embodied in the picture of a judge, courageous enough "to give the devil his due," whether he be in the right or in the wrong.* (*John F Dillon,* **The Laws and Jurisprudence of England and America** (Boston: Little, Brown and Company, 1894, p. 152.)

Similarly read Lord Justice Bowen:

> *..like my Brothers who sit with me, I am extremely reluctant to decide anything except what is necessary for the special case, because I believe by long experience that judgments come with far more weight and gravity when they come upon points which the Judges are bound to decide, and I believe that obiter dicta, like the proverbial bound to decide, and I believe that obiter dicta, like the proverbial chickens of destiny, come home to roost sooner or later in a very uncomfortable way to the Judges who have uttered them, and are a great source of embarrassment in future case. Therefore I abstain from putting a construction on more than it is necessary to do for this particular case.*
>
> *(Quote It-I p. 48 – L.J. Bowen).*

Obiter binds none, not even its author.

14

Crorepatis and Criminals—The Nihilistic Parliamentarians

Now that election has become a proximate, profound issue decisive of the nation's future, with creative potential for India's democratic survival, any improvement of the people's participative and representative character of the polls has a positive value and is welcome. To reduce the tension after the poll process is over and before the procedure for counting is concluded in a populous parliamentary constituency an alternative suggestion or proposal for eliminating delay and foul play and malpractice with ballots is called for.

What I suggest is the following :

When Mrs. Bhutto was the candidate in Pakistan's general elections several years ago after Zia's dictatorship but last I happened to be an international observer. Of course, there were other leading figures from other countries too. To my surprise, I found two novel features which we may copy with modification as felt necessary. One was that instead of the *local police*, to keep law and order, there were pickets of *army* people located some distances away from the polling station. I asked why the local police was kept away and the army was brought in? The reply was the local political leaders can influence the local police while the army cannot be. The second feature was phenomenal. At 5.00 p.m., when the polling ended, I went to the station. The returning officer told me that the counting in that polling station would begin at 7 p.m., a couple of hours later and each candidate's representative will be present at the counter when objections could be raised and considered by the returning officer. The result of the counting will be communicated to the candidates officially. This is decentralization of counting and quick results known to the nation. So much so, there was no tension or speculation and by late night from the various polling stations information will be available about the result of the counting. The victory of the candidate was not in doubt; no tampering in the polling station or while the boxes are in transit to the Central Polling Station was possible. This procedure will quicken the completion of the process, reduce tension and delay and the counting is easier, the number being manageable and the entire outfit at the polling booths will handle the counting effectively.

The second suggestion is what I thought was working well in the Soviet Union under the election law. Every large hospital and large prison had a small polling station. It may not be possible for many patients in the hospital to move to the polling station. But they can vote safely if inside the hospital there is a polling station with the candidates or their representative's presence like in any other polling station ensuring fair play. Many patients who otherwise cannot vote because of illness prevents them reaching from their polling station will be able to exercise their franchise by this harmless process. Similarly, Central prisons in every State keep in their custody thousands of under-trials otherwise entitled to vote. They cannot vote because they happen to be in custody though may perhaps, after trial, be acquitted. Why deny vote to those who are entitled to vote under the law by setting up a polling station in the prison. He was enabled to vote though for the time being he happens to be in custody. They should not be deprived of their right to choose a representative. This means that the candidate in custody who has a national franchise can elect his representative. Similarly, another suggestion is that every voter must have the right to suggest a name which he chooses for casting his vote if otherwise he finds difficult conscientiously to vote for all or any candidates as he finds them too bad to claim his approval. This too is a practice which, once prevailed in the Soviet Union.

The Law Reforms Commission - Kerala has made certain proposals which are akin to what has been stated above. Those proposals are reproduced below:

Amendment to Kerala Panchayath Raj Act

Amendment to Sec. 21. - In section 21 of the principal Act, after sub-section (2), the following explanation shall be added, namely:-

Explanation: A person who is detained as an undertrial prisoner in a jail or in custody of police or any other agency or as an in patient in any hospital shall be considered as a person absenting himself temporarily from his residence.

Amendment to Sec. 76. - In section 76 of the principal Act, in sub-section (5), for the words "or otherwise or in the lawful custody of the Police", the words "for a period more than one year or for an offence involving moral turpitude" shall be substituted.

Amendment to Kerala Municipalities Act

Amendment to Sec. 77. - In Section 77 of the Kerala Municipalities Act 1994 (hereinafter referred to as the Principal Act), after sub-section (2) the following explanation shall be added, namely:

> "Explanation: a person who is detained as an under trial prisoner in a jail or is in the custody of police or any other agency or as an in patient in any hospital shall be considered as a person absenting himself temporarily from his place of residence."

Amendment of Section 132. - In section 132 of the principal Act, in sub-section (5), for the words "or otherwise, or is in the lawful custody of the Police", the words "for a period more than one year or for an offence involving moral turptitude" shall be substituted.

In a State where parties are corrupt and candidates manipulate and win election through money, muscle and mafia power, each voter will no longer be disappointed, given the freedom to choose his candidate and cast his vote for him provided the ballot paper contains an extra column for the voter to cast his vote beyond the names formally printed in the ballot paper.

The process may be cumbersome but is a check on corruption or mafia manipulation of candidates and ensures freedom of franchise instead of being forced to choose one among the party chosen rotten apples. A propaganda move by the media and other publicity measure may make this procedure available for promoting clean elections. These suggestions require national debate and parliamentary legislation. I hope the nation will see some sense in the proposals I have made not with dogmatic originality but from what I have observed working elsewhere as satisfactory. The purpose is to see that democratic governance operates through candidates who effectively represent the constituency better than at present.

Indian humanity consists half of the women and if democracy is to have sex egalite and women power with its real play in the governance of the country every political party contesting elections should provide half the number of candidates from women. We find a gross disproportion in the presence of women in the judiciary, the legislature and the executive. This gender injustice can be corrected only by the Election Commission insisting on every political party seeking to contest the election providing the Election Commission with the candidates list of which half the number should be women. Or there must be more of constituency exclusively for women like the SC/ST at present. There can be a provision to make women's egalitarian participation by extensive reservation of constituencies for women only. Moreover, women must have the free choice to undergo family planning or ovarian removal without the husband's consent and the State make its facilities free for women to bear children or not to. Masculine domination in this area is a delicate issue but in the Soviet Union, Lenin had claimed that women will be free only if their right to sex is free. This requires some complicated infrastructure. But if we mean business and consider women's freedom seriously, we have to make necessary provisions in the law to make our intention real and achieve our goal.

Another provision which we may profitably consider borrowing from the Soviet election law is the right to recall an elected candidate for gross misconduct, for grave corruption or outrageous communalism. In the Soviet Union I have read such a provision exists and works. It is reported that party candidates have been successfully recalled on appropriate motion and subject to strict procedure. In India, today, corruption and communalism and other vices in elections and later by parliamentarians have reached Himalayan proportions that in extreme cases of proved misbehaviour is unworthy of members. There is no justification why a right of statutory recall should not be made under the Representation of People's Act. I seriously suggest that there is a National debate on this subject and, the recall, becomes a voter's right from panchayats to Parliament.

15

The Sri Lankan Tragedy

History and Geography, legend and religion, language and culture, commerce and ethnic pluralism, common imperial subjection and a host of human factors have brought India and Sri Lanka close together dating from the distant past and bound the people in a brotherhood by the mystic chords of memory and community of interest, beliefs and ways of life. What a lovely island, Sir Lanka, a paradise on earth, if only Tamils and Simhalas, in warm embrace, strove to build that blessed piece of earth God's best! What a hallowed country, India, where the Buddha was born, Tamil culture flourished and the Himalayas and the Ganga made the land and its people celestial and enriched the world with the highest peaks of philosophic thought and lofty literature. Two neighbours under imperial yoke! The British having left, the two countries should have redeemed their tryst with destiny and developed their economies and ties of friendship to mutual benefit. But alas, the internal problems of Colombo and Delhi defeated the expectations of the respective people; and the relations between the two countries did not run smooth either. India-Lanka friendship, so natural and beautiful, soured over the decades and, more importantly, stresses and strains within the Republics added to the estrangement. Democracy failed to fulfill its social and cultural promise in Sri Lanka when its finer essence of fraternity was fatally stabbed by the mechanics of majority rule, ethnic-linguistic bellicosity and the resurrection of the Buddha and Shiva to engage in power struggles!

Sri Lanka has a substantial minority of Tamils, mostly Hindu, inhabiting the North and East of the Island. The overwhelming majority is Simhala Buddhist plus there is a small Muslim population and some Christian presence too. The preponderant majority (Simhala Buddhist) is preferentially treated under the Constitution. In this pluralist society, Independence broke up human solidarity and political power grab gave rise to bleeding frictions. The Government, in the unitary Constitution of Sri Lanka, indulged in discrimination between the Tamils and the Simhalas to such an extent that periodic violence broke out, even the security for life and limb of the minority was in peril. The wild weeds of friction grew invisibly and happy fraternity became the first casualty.

Several attempts were made by India to solve the problems of the Tamils, but the Tamils' expectations darkened into anxiety, anxiety into dread and dread into battle for survival. They complained of State terrorism and Simhala macabre behaviour. The savage in man silences the angel in him when hateful situations show up.

The minorities were tortured and threatened, maimed and murdered, fled the Island and sought refuge in India and many other parts of the world. This minority was once politically significant, talent-wise resourceful and educationally advanced. Bitterness bred core groups 'red in tooth and claw' who began to fight back. Moderates fail when their counsel is hardly heeded by their followers who are besieged by majoritarians gone haywire! The broad picture was one of terrible violation of human rights of the Tamils, who were formally equal citizens under the Constitution. Prime Minister Indira Gandhi tried to produce harmony and made various proposals through her emissaries like G. Parthasarathi.

With Madras as headquarters an organization for the protection of human rights in Sri Lanka was formed, with me as President and Sri Rudramoorthy, an Advocate in Sri Lanka (a refugee in Madras) as Secretary. A distinguished panel of members were on the Committee like :

1. Dr. Upendra Baxi

   Vice-Chancellor, University of South Gujarath, Surat, Later Vice-Chancellor, Delhi University.

2. Mr. Nikhil Chakravarthy, Editor "Mainstream", Delhi.

3. Mr. Subrata Roy Chowdhury, Senior Advocate, Calcutta.
4. Prof. N. R. Madhava Menon
   Professor of Criminal Law, University of Delhi
   Director, National Law School University, Bangalore.
5. Prof. T. S. Rama Rao
   Professor of International and Constitutional Law, University of Madras, (now retired).
6. Mr. T. R. Ramaswamy, Editor, "News Today", Madras
7. Prof. J. N. Saxena,
   Professor of International Law, University of Delhi.
8. Dr. Soli J. Sorabjee
   Senior Advocate, Supreme Court of India; and formerly Attorney General of India.
9. Mr. N. T. Vanamamalai, Senior Advocate High Court of Madras.

Indeed, Sri Shankar Dayal Sharma was persuaded by me in the early eighties to be associated with this Human Rights Organisation. He became our sublime Head of State, Rashtrapatiji.

The letters written by me to Indiraji sum up the human rights scenario in Sri Lanka in 1984. I quote the letters in extenso as they project the grim picture in its gory colour.

1. Letter dated 10th August 1984 to the Prime Minister:

Madam Prime Minister,

I write this letter as President of the Organisation for the Protection of Human Rights in Sri Lanka. Right at the outset, I must record my appreciation of the concern you have expressed for the ethnic minority in Sri Lanka whose story of blood, toil, tears and sweat has become aggravated into a maaro scale human tragedy. State terrorism, I am sad to say, has been unleashed on an innocent civilian population identified culturally, ethnically, linguistically and otherwise as the Tamils of that Island. Even the alibi of violence on the part of some desperate, misguided Tamil extremists experimenting with a brutal short-cut (which history has proved is a wrong cult) cannot, by any stretch of exaggeration, be a justification for the massive, macabre and systematic barbarity practised by the forces of Law and Order, of the Navy and the Army under the control of the Sri Lanka State. These heinous excesses have resulted, according to reports reaching the Indian shores, in the shooting of Tamils, shelling of their houses, killing people in the streets, and so on. What happened in July 1983 seems to be part of a process which is being continued ever since without abatement; with the result that a fifth of the total population of the Island of Sri Lanka (constituted by the Tamils there) is now in mortal fear of their very security and survival.

It is obvious, without more argument, that the human rights of these brothers and sisters are in grave peril. After all, the Tamils of Sri Lanka are part of the human family of the Planet Earth. We must recognise the indivisibility of justice and human rights as part of civilised international jurisprudence. Butchery in Jaffna is tragedy in India! Gandhiji and Pandit Nehru bequeathed to us these human values which find expression in international law. A grievous wrong done to any one anywhere is a gory blow to everyone everywhere. As a leader of the Non- Aligned Movement with its commitment to peace, as Prime Minister of India, with its deep constitutional humanism, and as a leading figure in world politics and of the United Nations which demands respect for human rights in the member countries, it is but appropriate that you take recourse to the accepted principles in International Law of peaceful humanitarian intervention. The plea of Domestic Jurisdiction and Internal Soveringnty has its limitations in a world woven into one, and these terms of legal diction and political connotation have a contemporary relativity which permit Indian presence and your persuasion in the poignant Human Rights Situation in Sri Lanka, the land where Lord Buddha has official pre-eminence but his Karuna is on a long holiday! I do not even hint at coercion by India, but the dynamics of escalating tumult and explosive torture in the neighbourhood may develop beyond our reckoning.

India is a neighbour of Sri Lanka with but a few miles of water separating us. Even otherwise, our country's security and proximity with Sri Lanka create a nexus, our history and culture bring us closer together. Our mutual concerns cannot be ignored and our obvious bonds need no explanation. All that I wish to emphasise is that Indian feeling over the human rights of Sri Lanka's minority is natural and inevitable.

You have so often made it abundantly clear that India's intentions are purely confined to helping Sri Lanka solve its problems vis-a-vis the Tamil minority there. Essentially, it is their problem; but you have often indicated that India is keen to see Sri Lanka settle this problem of Tamil minority justly. What unsettles Sri Lanka has its strong ripples in India.

While I am concerned with one facet only of the larger issues surrounding the problems of Tamils, viz. their human rights, I draw your attention to the grave crisis which is developing in Jaffna and other areas of Tamil habitation in recent days. The bleeding tale of human brutality, from a purely human rights angle, has reached a stage where I wish you expressed in clear tones and imperative voice the world's concern for the life and lot of the minority in Sri Lanka now under harassment by the Defence Forces themselves. My appeal to you, on behalf of the Organisation over which I preside pro tem, is to use your great good office, through appropriate diplomatic and other channels, to impress upon Sri Lanka's President that his Government cannot get away with it, if a substantial minority in his country is subjected to the inhumanity of torture and death and destruction of property by the State's own Forces.

2. Letter dated 17th September 1984 to the Prime Minister

I write this letter to convey to you my deep

appreciation of the stand you have taken on behalf of the Indian people in the matter of the Tamils of Sri Lanka. It is so heartening to hear from your authoritative voice that our entire Nation is with Sri Lanka Tamils. I further agree with your right emphasis on the Human Rights issue. They are Tamils, they are our neighbours. But the crucial question is not solidarity with Tamils qua Tamils nor as people in India's proximity because of location. Intense identity with the Human Rights of this Minority is very much in tune with our concerns. There is an indivisibility about Human Rights which drives the Indian people to the aid of Sri Lanka's Tamils as common tenants of the earth.

As the President of the Organisation for the Protection of Human Rights in Sri Lanka, I express my gratitude once again.

At a certain stage, I sent a cable to the International Committee of the Red Cross which brings out the bleeding exasperation and deprivation of the Island's Tamil population.

Cable dated 8th August 1984 to the International Committee of the Red Cross, Geneva

Pray rush rescue measures and humanitarian intervention for Sri Lanka Tamils. Defence forces shot and killed hundreds of innocent Tamil civilians, destroyed numerous Tamil houses by shelling civilian residences from the sea and numerous fishing boats sunk. Thousands rendered destitute and fleeing for shelter and food. Dead bodies lying strewn on roads, people in terror. Red cross must urgently send help I beseech your immediate measures to save Tamils from dead and distress.

Meanwhile, reports of brutality and commission of genocide came from various sources like Law Asia and other reputed international bodies. A Commission of high stature to enquire into the grievous violations of human rights in the Island - rape, murder, loot etc., was sought to be sent out but could not take off; and even a visit by me heading a team, including Sri Sachar (former Chief Justice and PUCL Chief), could not be made because visas were not granted by Colombo. Republica, turned despotic, reject audit. Even so, many well-attended public meetings were held in Tamil Nadu and New Delhi, explaining to Indians the harrowing conditions of Tamils in Sri Lanka and the barbarity, with pogrom pattern and Hitlerite methodology, adopted by Simhala chauvinists and the Jayawardane (J.R.J.) Government. I used to meet Sri Amritalingam in Madras. He was an outstanding political leader who had sought asylum in India. What a gentle soul who liked Prabhakaran but was later assassinated treacherously by his men! Other sober leaders like Sivasubramaniam also used to give me details of horrendous happenings of massacres even in hospitals across the Palk Strait.

I remember how Rudramurthi, the Secretary of the Organization, fainted in tears at meetings while painting, with a bleeding heart, the terrorist malevolence and traumatic victimisation for which the J.R.J. regime, and Simhala goons unbridled, were responsible. A satanic divide, with militant cohorts of Simhala Buddhists suddenly turning brutish and abetted by the State itself, made the island republic quasifascist. Sweet Ceylon, lovely and green, with high literacy and Hindu-Buddhist-Muslim-Christian amity, became the graveyard of humanism and compassion under the malignant cult of Simhala raj. May be, historically, the Tamils had a larger share of the cake to begin with. But political cunning and calculated conditioning of ethnic-linguistic-monkistic culture spread hatred on fascis lines. God is Mercy but godism can be macabre under the spell of cannibal cults and hatreds! J.R.J. was a subtle, able, pious and charismatic leader who could play the feuhrer adroitly, with a civilised veneer. Himself a compassionate soul perhaps, his regime veered to fascist ways.

Bertrand Russel says somewhere:

> "The first step in a fascist movement, is the combination under an energetic leader of a number of men who possess more than the average share of leisure, brutality, and stupidity. The next step is to fascinate fools and muzzle the intelligent, by emotional excitement on the one hand and terrorism on the other."

When religious obscurantism is superadded inhumanity becomes cankerous.

The wave of violence engineered by the State-Buddhist operators was not openly resisted by a large section of democratic people, perhaps out of fear. Colombo, a beautiful city with the Supreme Court and Presidential Palace, did nothing to arrest the dangerous trend. Silence is sin where protest is the test of conscience.

Anyway, hatred begets hatred, violence provokes violence; Hitlerism breeds Hitlerism and despair midwifes desparate broods. Thus were born the Tamil militants. Many groups sprang from the Jaffna soil. Bitter and brutal were their reprisals, and Indira's India helped with training these new brands of youth, more to neutralise attacks than to ignite insatiable terrorism. Indeed, the Tamil demand was not a separate sovereign state but honour, autonomy and justice, political, social and economic. But history tells us that when justice is met with injustice, human rights with inhumanity, autonomy with autocracy and democracy with fascist tactics, oppressed people choose the gun; and that is the demographic, demoguogic cradle of terrorism. And thus arose the Tamil Tigers and their feuhrer Prabhakaran. A dialectical key to history opens the mystery of the L.T.T.E. and their counter-savagery. Given credible negotiations and basic decencies and good offices of India and the international community Tamil-Simhala accord and constitutional concord possible, feasible.

India had problems in the Punjab and, naturally, was not willing to aid any secessionist demand. But Indiraji made many efforts, with diplomatic limitations, to secure political justice and State autonomy for the Tamils. The world over, the progressives sympathised with the suppressed Tamils. I remember addressing a few meetings in Europe, London and New York explaining the just demands of the Tamils but not the break-up of the Republic.

By way of divagation but with deep relevance to the issues of schism and secessionism and follow-up of savage struggles, let me quote a letter from a knowledgeable Tamil with Sri Lankan roots.

Letter dated 18th July 1984 from Mr. N. Nayagam, Advocate, Madurai

Dear Justice V. R. Krishna Iyer,

I have read your article under the heading "Sri Lanka Tamils" which appeared in the *Hindu* on the 16th instant with great delight and interest. At the same time I also read the views expressed by the Deputy High Commissioner of Sri Lanka in India, Mr. Priyasena in the issue of the *Hindu* of the 18th instant.

I am very anxious to furnish you certain authoratative information regarding his reputations, which I am sure, you will accept with great satisfaction.

I am an Indian citizen, having resided in Sri Lanka for well over 35 years, studied and graduated in law there, practised as an Attorney-at-law for over 20 years and migrated to my country, and I am practising as an Advocate in Madurai. I am quite conversant with all past and present political affairs concerning the Tamils and the deception and disappointments perpetrated by successive Simhalese Governments on the innocent law-abiding Tamil people of Sri Lanka. I am very anxious to meet you in person and enlighten you on various matters concerning Sri Lankan affairs.

In this context, I wish to furnish below the following:

1. President J.R. Jayavardene was the person who

proposed the resolution to make Simhala the office language of the country at the U.N.P. Convention held at Kelaniya in the year 1953. This resolution was later introduced in the form of a Bill called "The Simhala only Bill" in parliament by the late S W R D Bandaranaike, and it became law. This controversial legislation sowed the seeds of discord between the Simhalese and the Tamil community who had been living in complete aminity and friendship hitherto.

2. After the first communal riots in 1958 following the vehement agitation by the Tamils over the passing of the 'Simhala only' bill, an agreement was reached between the late Mr. S J V Chelvanayakam, Q.C., leader of the Federal party (called in Tamil as Ilankai , Tamil Arasu Kadchi) and the late Mr. S W R D Bandaranaike, the then Prime Minister of Ceylon. This pact was called the BC pact or the Banda-chelva pact which provided for inter-alia, the establishment of Regional Councils in the 22 Districts of Ceylon. This pact was to be drafted in the form of a Bill and introduced in Parliament. Important: At this time, J.R. Jayavardene's U.N.P. party had only eight M.Ps in parliament and he, of all persons, took out a padayatra from Kelaniya (then his constituency) to Kandy. This padayatra was stopped halfway by the Banda Government. Being disappointed, he instigated the Buddhist clergy to protest against the implementation of the pact and the Buddhist

bhikkus performed satyagraha in front of Mr. Bandaranaike's house and the pact was abrogated. Had this pact seen the light of day, the present ills of the Tamils would have been solved then. But it did not so. After 25 years, Sri Lanka is still unable to solve this tangle. So who is responsible for this malady? Why is it that Mr. Jayawardene did this dirty thing? It was because he never wanted to have this Tamils issue settled as this was a trump card for successive Simhalese Governments to come to power through the hustings.

3. Please bear in mind that it was the U.N.P which was responsible for the attempted coup-de-tat of 1971. They wanted to capture power and they pre-arranged to overthrow the democratically constituted Government of Bandaranaike. Prior to that, they with the help of Buddharakhita Thers, the High Priest of the Kelaniya Buddhist temple, "bumped off" the late Mr. S.W.R.D. Bandaranaike, and implicated the innocent Soma Rama Thers, alleged assailant, who was hanged. The High Priest of Kelaniya was the right-hand man of Mr. Jayavardene.

So from the above facts, can you imagine for a moment that President Jayavardene will solve the ethnic problem of Sri Lanka at the Round Table Conference which now in session? He is dead against conceding Regional Councils which were contemplated as far back as 1958 as he thinks that it will be a prelude to separation.

The idea for separation was never mooted by either the All Ceylon Tamil Congress or the Federal party. It was originally mooted by Mr. C. Santhanalingam, the second of the famous Lingam brothers, the eldest being Justice Nagalingam Q.C. who retired as Senior Justice and acted as the Governor General of Ceylon once. His other brother was the late Mr. C. Thiagalingam Q.C. This Santhanalingam passed the I.C.S. and the C.C.S. and later became the first Professor of Mathematics of Ceylon University and was the first Minister of Trade and Commerce in the first coalition ministry formed by the First Prime Minister of Independent Ceylon. Such a man predicted that the only alternative and the salvation of the Tamils lay in separation. At that time, the A.C.T. Congress and the Federal Party laughed at his idea and nicknamed him as a “buffoon”. Now the T.M.L.F. or rather the entire Tamil nation is crying for separation.

Who responsible for this cry for separation? It is the successive Simhalese governments. Who is responsible for the growing of terrorism and the springing of terrorists? There again it is the Government of Sri Lanka. Any majority Government must concede or rather fulfil the aspirations of the minority. This is the most fundamental principle of democracy. The disgruntled and the ever disappointed educated youths of the Tamils have thought it wise to launch their struggle to liberate their traditional homeland of “Eelam”. There is nothing wrong in their adopting guerilla warfare and forcing pressure on the Government to concede their demands.

As to the examples cited by Mr. Priyasena regarding personalities being "bumped off" just because they were joining the mainstream of the national of the Government, I like to elucidate further on this matter. The late Mr. Alfred T. Duraiappah, Mayor and twice M.P. for Jaffna was really "bumped off" as he was an opportunist and a fifth columnist. Similarly the late Mr. A. Thiagarajah was shot by the terrorist first to get rid of another opportunist who was trying to be a traitor to the Tamils by winning favours for himself and his coterie from the Simhalese Government. Thus you would see that the idea behind bumping off of these personalities was to bring in unity among the Tamils. Disunity, I admit, among the Tamils was one of the main causes for their weakness and failure of parleys and discussions with the Centre. In Sri Lanka, you find the Cinnamon Garden Tamils, who were and still the supporters of any Simhalese Government and first to win favours from it. Then you find the upcountry Tamils (the Tamils of Indian origin) who came to the island as plantation labourers. Again there are the Jaffna Tamils, who are subject to Thesavalamai, a system of law prevalent in Ceylon, and applicable to the Malabar inhabitants of Jaffna. You also find the Batticaloa Tamils from the Eastern Province. The Muslims in Ceylon also speak Tamil and their mother tongue is Tamil. They too form the mainsteam of the Tamils but they always join any Simhalese Government which comes to power in order to win their favours.

President Jayavardene has absolutely no intention

to settle the demands of the Tamils though he cannot brush aside the good offices offered by the Prime Minister of India to settle this ethnic problem.

Recently I had been to Jaffna and I saw the destruction caused to buildings belonging to the Tamils and the Simhalese as a result of the violence and I was able to see a certain amount of fear and panic prevailing there. The town looks deserted as people wish to seek safety by confining themselves to their houses.

In my opinion the problem of the Tamils will not be solved by the Jayawardene Government or by any Simhalese Government as they do not want to concede any of the demands of the Tamils. Therefore, only foreign intervention (which is not possible) will be able to solve the problem. In which case Sri Lanka, I think will fall into the hands of any Superpower and that will be America.

I am furnishing this letter of information to you so that, if you desire, you may suitably reply to the observations put forward by Mr. Priyasena in the light of the points furnished by me.

I wish to meet you and discuss further on this matter. Please write to me so that I can communicate with you in future.

A glimpse of the agony of Jaffna is gained from a letter I wrote to the International Committee of the Red Cross Switzerland on 30th July, 1984.

Letter dated 30th July 1984 sent to the International Committee of the Red Cross, Switzerland

Dear Sir,

The physical and mental torture, the genocidal and the allied operation which have become a terrible fact of life for the Tamils of Sri Lanka, have been attested to by various International Organisations with concern for Human Rights. The International Red Cross has always hurried to the humanitarian rescue of persons and groups which have been victimised by violence and worse in war and other gruesome mass situations. The ethnic minority called the Tamils of Sri Lanka are distressed about their present and future and apprehend daily the attacks by hoodlums from the majority community - Simhalese. On top of that, the State apparatus, consisting of the police and the army, is directly and indirectly operating to inflict destruction of life and property on Sri Lankan Tamils.

They are a minority entitled to protection in any civilised democracy, but they have been denied it. Even basic security, what with the bloodbath of July 1983 and after, is absent. They are helpless, precarious and do not have any rescue when set upon by groups from the majority community and Units of the Armed Forces of the State. Dead bodies lie in the streets because of the relatives of the dead are afraid to go near for fear of being killed. Medical help appears to be a theoretical prospect, what with murders of Tamils even in hospitals. Indeed, investigation by the Amnesty International, by the Minority Rights Group, by the Law Asia Human Rights Standing Committee and the like, have a sad tale to tell. The Tamils of Sri Lanka, even if they be regarded as extremists of guerillas - this is an exaggeration and caricature and substantial untruth, save for a small group of desparate young persons - are entitled to protection and rescue by your humane Organisation, the Red Cross. The times are critical according to reports trickling into South India from Sri Lanka, and Tamils are in mortal peril. Assuming that the truth is only a fraction of what I have said above, even then the Red Cross, in its humane orbit, must intervene with the Sri Lanka President and seek to help those who are subjected to violence and killing and other forms of unbearable cruelty.

I write this letter as President of an Organisation called "Organisation for the Protection of Human Rights in Sri Lanka". May I request you to extend your Organisation's benign help to the minority community of Tamils in Sri Lanka?

History never stands still. Sometimes it makes a quantum leap, but such jumps are fed by silent developments of sorrows and suppressions, determined resistance and organised opposition. Therefore, to grasp the power of the LTTE, its bitter, bloodthirsty barbarity (no alibi) and the final goal of human liberation, there must be willingness to follow the intermediate events, now visible, now invisible, now terrorist, and now crushed. From this perspective, please read a resolution of the O P H R S L.

DRAFT RESOULTION

A. The Executive Committee of the Organisation for the Protection of Human Rights in Sri Lanka records its profound concern for the human rights of the Sri Lanka Tamil minority, protests strongly against the genocidal aggression on their very survival and safety and condemns the barbaric torture unleashed on them by the Government and violent Simhalese gang-ups.

B. This Committee takes a grave view of the Sri Lanka President's dangerous project of bringing into the Island the notorious Mossad of Israel with its international record of human rights butchery and anti-Islamic terrorism, and condemns without reservations the repressive violence let loose on the Moors and their basic rights. Furthermore, this Committee regards with shock the unblushing measure of President Jayawardane to hire British mercenaries (the S A S) for brutally crushing the minorities (Tamils and Moors) and the radical Simhalese students.

We view with consternation the disingenuous moves of the Island Government to facilitate American naval presence by proxy and other guises the vicious impact of which will go beyond its boundaries and inject a new threat to peace in the region and destabilisation potential in the Indian Ocean community of nations.

Rejecting, in the specific circumstances, the alibi urged by the Island's President of 'Internal matter' and domestic jurisdiction as invalid in international law, this committee makes common case with Tamils and Moors, radical students and progressive Sinhalese in defence of human rights now under violent threat from the Head of State and his forces, and appeals to the U.N. organs, the international comity of nations, all lovers of human rights everywhere and many enlightened Simhala brothers and sisters to raise their collective voice against the growing menace to Freedom and Peace.

Then came Rajiv Gandhi after the Indira assassination, who too showed concern for the human rights of the Tamils in Sri Lanka. The O P H R S L invoked his humanist disposition through the following letter dated 6th November, 1984.

Dear Sri Rajiv Gandhi,

I write this letter on behalf of myself and as President of 'Organisation for the Protection of Human Rights in Sri Lanka' to express the profound sorrow of the large number of refugees from Sri Lanka whose human rights have been travestied and trampled upon in their own country and on behalf of all those in India who support the cause of the Tamils in Sri Lanka. Smt. Indira Gandhi, as Prime Minister of India and as a world leader, had done her best, within the frame-work of the hard realities of international law and life, to do her utmost to secure for Sri Lankan Tamil millions the basic rights which had been denied to them. The Organisation of which I am the President, and which represents in large measure the agony of the traumatised Tamils, is deeply distressed by the sudden and shocking death of one who, Mrs. Gandhi at national and international levels, gave tongue to the toils and tears of the ethnic minority of Indian origin, oppressed and suppressed that you and your Government will take a clear and firm line in defence of the numberless Srilankans, called the Tamil minority, currently facing indescribable torture, tantruma and state terrorism.

Prime Minister Rajiv, sometimes young and rash, impatient and impetuous, arrogant and imperious, took some steps, through sea and air, to help besieged Jaffna, starved of food and medicine by a heartless Buddhist President J.R.J. The canny Sri Lankan head of State tempted Rajiv, an infant of vanity in diplomacy, into an Indo-Sri Lanka Accord. Rajiv felt inflated into a world figure and visited Colombo and quickly signed the Treaty which contained clauses too tricky for the Indian to grasp. This was the beginning of the end of goodwill between Jaffna and Delhi except for some quislings. I have no doubt that the Lankan Tamils were the best friends of India and were anti-imperialist in essence. By a curious distortion of truth and a failure to explain to the Simhala people India's abundant goodwill and cultural relations with Sri Lanka, a widespread hostility, mistrust and suspicion about Indian intentions infiltrated the minds of Simhalas and the Buddhist monks. **Suspicion is the upas tree under whose shade reason fails and justice dies.** It is most unfortunate that while Buddhism would have been a strong bond between the two people, the Monastery politics polluted the cordial relations.

A great tribute needs to be paid to the Christian Church. The message of Jesus was love, humanism and the redemption of the weak and the humble, using spiritual healing. The church in the Island is not numerically strong, but by their work of compassion, education, and service to society, has a hold on the hearts of the people and a voice which commands the respect of the authorities. All their human resources were devoted to bringing about peace and settlement, with justice and Charity even as the struggle between JRJ's army and Prabhakaran's hordes resulted in continuing bloodshed, ghastly and indefensible. The church persisted undaunted in India and Sri Lanka to foster rapproachement through formulas acceptable to both sides. However, a solution has baffled all of us, innocent blood is being split even to-day. Treachery and mistrust are infecting the air and God's work, the Jesus mission, the Buddha's compassion, and Shiva's supreme power for good in the Island humanity is still a teasing illusion and promise of unreality.

In Hong Kong, when a group including me, met, specific constitutional recommendations emerged in the light of discussions held in a friendly atmosphere. Earlier, the Indo-Sri Lanka Friendship Society, with me as patron, had drafted a detailed proposal. However, the end is not in sight. Perhaps, in Churchill's words:

"This is not the end. It is not even the beginning of the end. But it is, perhaps, the end of the beginning."

We can never give up the effort to humanise Sri Lanka. A great people with cultural pluralism and structural federalism have a tryst with destiny which remains to be redeemed. All humanity is one. True nationalism is intense internationalism. Violence must stop on both sides, lest the worst should happen. "Whoever fights monsters should see to it that in the process he does not become a monster. And when you look long into an abyss, the abyss also looks long into you". - NIETZSCHE.

A new world human order is unfolding although killings and corpses mar the course. We must conscientise ourselves to produce a new harmony among the Sri Lankans - Tamils and Simhalese.

"In the cause of freedom we have to battle for the right of people with whom we do not agree; and whom, in many cases, we may not like ... If we do not defend their rights, we endanger our own."

Harry Truman.

In the hope that good begets good and love love, we must appeal to the Sri Lankan brotherhood to live together, respect each other, forget the past and establish a new quasi-federal camaraderie.

There are legal tools for transformation. There are military moves for victory, but the healing touch must come from the heart, from love, in its extra-ordinary paradox of conquest, as G.K. Chesterton has felicitously expressed:

"Loving means to love that which is unlovable,
Or it is no virtue at all.
Forgiving means to pardon the unpardonable,
Faith means believing the unbelievable,
And hoping means to hope when things are hopeless."

I have still hopes that despite the savage exchanges between the Tamil Tigers, and the military terrorists, there can be truce, followed by peace, followed by fraternity. I have had occasion to meet a LTTE Central Committee member Thilagar in London many years ago. He seems to reflect the view of the LTTE that friendly relations with India were a necessity of the South-East Asian region. I had met the 'late' Kittu in Madras and he had impressed me with his earnestness for peace with India and Colombo and for cease-fire with the IPKF. He was constructive in his approach and was wanting to persuade Prabhakaran to surrender weapons to the IPKF, but this pacifism of Kittu was shot down while his messenger was moving to meet Prabhakaran. Even as I was shocked, Amirthalingam was treacherously killed by the Tigers. I was shaken when Kittu was recently "killed" while returning to Jaffna with secret peace proposals allegedly approved by unnamed European Governments.

"Others say Kittu had a more personal mission. Some of his thinking had changed in four years of exile and he wanted Prabhakaran to know how the ruthless inward-looking Tiger movement was perceived by over 250,000 Tamil refugees in Europe. He also believed that if the Tamil liberation struggle

was to be successful in the long term it must win acceptance from the international community and observe international human rights standards. Thousands gathered for a massive three-day hartal or protest in Jaffna after his death and there were LTTE-organised demonstrations in London, Paris and New York. In the aftermath, the only certainty is that the Tigers will strike back, probably at Indian interests."

Kittu was a humane person whose presence, if "alive" would have catalyzed the process of peace-making. Prabhakaran himself was not, perhaps, as vicious as is projected by Colombo. Such persons are the product of misrule and mis-appropriation of state power. Hitler himself was a Satanic eruption of the post-World War I injustices. In a most controversial statement with a core of truth and evil exaggerations, Winston Churchill said (Of course, before World War II):

He (Hitler) embodied the revolt of Germany against the hard fortunes of war ... Adolf Hitler is Fuehrer because he exemplifies and enshrines the will of Germany.

The Sri Lanka Monitor in a recent issue states:

As the Kittu drama unfolded, Colombo's newly-installed Anglican Bishop, Rev Kenneth Fernando had just returned from a peace mission to Jaffna where he talked with Prabhakaran, the first time the elusive guerrilla leader had met with outsiders for almost two years. Bishop Fernando described Prabhakaran as a "humane man", kicking up a new dust storm in the colombopress, and called for a new inter-religious peace initiative. Prabhakaran released two of the 39 police men held by the Tigers into ICRC custody as a goodwill gesture and invited the Bishop to return to Jaffna with a delegation of southern "intellectuals".

Days later, another group of intellectuals convened by Colombo Tamil lawyer Neelan Tiruchelvam were briefed by Dayan Jayatilleka, one of President Premadasa's inner circle on the realities of the Government's room for manoeuvre over the peace issue.

"Devolution of power is a categorical imperative of Sri Lankan stability. The federal shape that must eventually be fashioned depends on the dialectics of Sri Lankan realities:

If Kittu's mission was peaceful in whatever sense, his death represents another lost opportunity to break down intransigence, polarisation and escalation on both sides. If Bishop Fernando's initiative has pricked the public conscience, more pressure must come for peace from both outside and inside Sri Lanka.

Let us never give up hope because the womb of the future will surely hold peace to be midwifed at the appropriate time by creative history. We must do our part. "There are no passengers on Spaceship Earth. Everybody's crew." **—Marshall Mcluhan.**

The exit of Rajiv and the entry of the Narasimha Rao have filled the hands of the Indian Prime Minister with a multitude of intractable internal problems and a humiliating role of financial medicancy. So much so, hardly anything is being done vis-a-vis Sri Lanka, Premadasa's visit notwithstanding. Things are dull and the Lanka desk is a vacuum in the Foreign Ministry. If ever the NAM and the SAARC of which India is a leader can play a part in shaping the Island's peaceful future, it is **NOW.** The Indian people have vicarious responsibility and regional concern. Therefore shall we give form and shape to Gandhiji's firm faith:

> "My nationalism is intense internationalism. I am sick of the strife between nations or religions."

16

Sports Development Sine Qua Non of National Advance

The right to life, guaranteed as fundamental in the pharmacopoeia of constitutional therapies against social, economic and other pathologies, is a paramount wonder of our Suprema Lex. Life survives only if humanity enjoys good health, physical, mental and moral. This dimension of Article 21 of the Constitution (Right to Life) demands the state's active promotion of sports and games and even yogic exercises so that an energetic generation may come to State away from sickness and ever spurred by Athletic proficiency. Sports and games have a glamour and a glory but in this commercialized universe of grammar, is reduced by gamble. Money power of Big Business monopolises the sports field by temptations and prizes and other attractive material. We need a healthy policy of the State vis a vis promotion of sports and games for the youth of both sexes. Long years ago when I was a young laywer, I was taking considerable interest in promotion of many games in my region of North Malabar. In seventies, when I became a minister in the Kerala State I became a senior member of the State Sports Council. Years passed and I was back at the Bar. My colleague in the Council of Ministers who later became a notable

Chief Minister was Sri. C. Achutha Menon. He was interested in development of games and sports in Kerala and left the need for evolving a sports policy for the State. So he requested me to prepare a report which could form the basis for the evolution of statutory foundation for sports and games. Meanwhile, I had become a judge of the Kerala High Court. Nevertheless I spared some time to oblige my close friend and then Chief Minister Achutha Menon. My report is that of a committee although the opening chapter includes my vision, as the inauguration of the committee's project. Times have changed but the spirit of sports is lottery wonder, integral to national development. What was a preliminary literature by me in the field of sports literature, still has relevance and so I enclose it for the wider audience of readership across the country followed by my introductory presentation of democratic development of health of the people. Yoga and scientific meditation are also complimentary to the right to life in good health.

Report of the Committee for the Better Development of Sports and Games in Kerala

We are living in a rapidly developing technological era where more muscular might of the human being may not spell defeat or victory in any department of activity, material or other. Nevertheless, the question of development of sports and games among student and not student youth has escalated in importance in our country as in others for, those qualities of physical fitness, discipline and leadership which are implied in the concept of sportsmanship, are called for in greater measure in these challenging times more than in the past. Viewed in this context, and having regard to the crores of rupees spent on education, it is but right to stress that physical education, understood in the widest sense, must be regarded as part of total education and be integrated with life at school and college and even outside the occupational hours of the youth of our land. Rightly, therefore, the Kerala Government, felt the need for the popular cultivation of those qualities essential for the balanced physical development of the human personality and the sports status of the youth of Kerala.

The whole object of sport is to promote the joy of life, as a virtue flowing from positive health. A touch of tradition – In the ages gone by Ayurveda stressed the sanctity of positive health – Arogyasutra more than prescribing procedures to cure diseases. Our ancients have said that for the practice of Dharma, Artha, Kama and Moksha the chief foundation is Arogya, which is physical well being or abundant health forming the basic pre-requisite for the blooming of other faculties, mental, moral or spiritual. As Dr. Radhakrishnan says, the Yoga Sutra "insists that physical prowess is essential. Rupa-lavanya-balavajrasamhanatvani kaya-sampath. Kaya-sampat or physical prowess consists in the development of rupa or beauty of form, lavanya or radiance, bala or strength, vajrasamhanatva, invulnerability like a diamond". The keynote of our humble report is therefore.

A Glance at some Ideological Aspects

We want more play fields now than copies of the Bhagavad Geetha, Swami Vivekananda is reported to have once saliently remarked. Swamiji is right today as in his day, for, our nation with all its traditions and talents can hardly hope to progress till its millions are physically healthy and strong. Thus, in national terms, we have to create a generation full of physical self-confidence, mental prowess, competitive skill and ability to win without losing one's and to lose without losing one's heart and to be gentlemen on and off the field. A true sportsmen is one who possesses, to adapt the grand Churchillian manner:

In war resolution; in defeat defines; in victory magnanimity, in peace goodwilll.

The desideratum is an awakening of the people to sports proficiency 'in widest commonalty spread'. The national goal must be: 'For every one a good physique, enjoyed through games and sports', and the national programme, the involvement of the entire able-bodied community in a comprehensive athletic programme. 'Operation Othenan', if I may so call this project, must naturally turn attention on youth, student and non-student, it must accelerate the sports activities of the many, more than emphasise the individual excellence of the few. Our object must be the creation of a wide base and systematic training rather than the crazy chase of precious metal at the next Asiad or Olympics.

We propose in this report to silhouette a Master Plan, informed, as in other national matters by Indian traditions, reasources and prospects, for the development of Sports and Games in Kerala. We regard it as a cultural effort which the state is obligated to make, on a scale unprecedented as it embraces the broad masses, and organised in a democratic way so that the Olympic spirit and the Arjun art will start at the grass roots and not be limited to the upper brackets of the sports elite.

The Soviet Experiment

If we study other countries which have been backward in sports games but have since forged strides, the demand for a dynamic and daring policy will be realised without much argument. This is the lesson we learn from Soviet experience. The webs in their famous book on the Soviet Civilisation have described the story thus:

> "Characteristically enough, in this story of the Remaking of Man, we have to begin with physical culture, in which the people of Tsarist Russia were exceptionally deficient. For the children of all ages... there is now-a-days nothing so universally taught, and so incessantly repeated, as training in the bodily habits that make for perfect health. In 1923 an All-Union Council for Physical Culture was established, consisting of representatives of the Trade Unions, the Communist Party and the Comsomols, on the one hand, and of the Commissariates of Education, Health and Defence. Under the influence of this Council, and largely at the expenses of the

commissariate of education of several constituent and autonomous republics, physical exercises of all kinds have been made the subject of repeated scientific investigation, and of literally hundreds of textbooks and treatises, which the state publishing enterprises have issued to the teachers in hundreds of thousands of copies: thus in numbers vastly exceeding those for Great Britain, Germany or the United States. For the adolescents an important channel of influence for both sexes is the rapidly growing young Communist League (Comsomols) now (1953) counting some five million members, mostly between 17 and 25. In every Comsomol cell the maintenance of perfect health is demanded from every member. Daily physical exercises become a social obligation, the fulfilment of which is urged every morning throughout the land by the innumerable loud speakers of the State radio service. But the most strifing manifestation of this 'universalism' in physical culture is the increase during the past few years in organised participation in every form of sports or games, from running, skating, ski-jumping, rowing, bicycling, fencing and gymnastic entertainments, to football, basketball, bowls, lawn tennis, baseball and folk-dancing. Three salient points strike the observer. One is the extent to which in the Soviet Union, all this cultivation of game and sport is consciously based on the conviction, in the young people themselves, that it promotes and maintains physical health and therefore constitutes a part of civil duty. Another is the close association, not only of physical exercises, but also of all organised games, with medical supervision and research. The third difference is the cordial encouragement, the co-operation and the financial subventions that are universally accorded to what has quickly become a national habit, not only by the people's Commissars of Education and Health in the various constituent and autonomous republics, but also by every government department that can be helpful". (pages 734 to 736).

By sheer national effort the Soviets have claimed an enviable place in the sports map of the world: of course, the U.S.A. too – with populations less than half of that of India. I stress Soviet conditions because they were very backward indeed under the Czars and made a poor international show till World War II. And yet their current achievements are spectacular enough for us to learn lessons. Every fourth or fifth Soviet citizen goes in for sports today. The sports societies in that country unite some two hundred thousand primary training clubs at factories and plants, at enterprises, educational establishments, at co-operative and state farms. Each of the national republics has its own trade union sports society. Moreover, each republic has its society for rural sportsmen. At their disposal the sportsmen have nearly 3000 stadiums, some 30,000 complex sports grounds, about 85,000 football fields, 36,000 gyms, over 7000, tourist bases and camps. Scores of cities have built sports places and indoor tracks. The work of all these sports societies is co-ordinated and headed by a public organisation – The Central Council of the Union of Sports/Societies and Organisations of the U.S.S.R. In the USSR there are three main sources for subsidizing sports – government allocations, trade union allocations and dues paid by the members of voluntary sports societies. The smallest part of the expenditure for sports is paid for out of the dues. A member of a voluntary sports society pays only 30 kopecks (33 us cents) a year in dues. In 1968 the Government allocated 7.6 thousand million roubles (1 rouble = 1.11 US dollars) for public health and sports. All athletes in the USSR, boxers included, do not pay a single kopeck for coaching or for the use of the gym. All boxing equipment, sports togs, medical advice are provided free of charge.

It is an axiomatic principle in the policy of a socialistic state that the population, especially the youth, should be given all-round encouragement in physical training and sports. Sports must really be a grass-roots' movement as it is in the USSR and some other countries. Its structure must be voluntary and democratic, its man power unlimited, its methods scientific and its material resource the onus of the State. If one may enunciate the principle accepted by the committee unanimously, all sports activity in the states should be organised by voluntary sports associations, including public organisations, based on the principles of self-management and statutory supervision wherever desirable and necessary. The activities of such sports societies should be co-ordinated, guided and controlled by a public organisation with statutory status which may roughly correspond to the present Kerala Sports Council. We visualise mass participation, and therefore mass trade union sports societies have an important role, whether the worker be in a farm or factory. Of course, student youth is the focus of attention not merely for practical but also for theoretical and scientific training. It is not, therefore inappropriate to include in the school curricula, lessons in sports, so that while training is being imparted and talented and persevering youngsters are given fillip, the progress may be according to scientific techniques. In short, while the Olympic principle will be the guiding star of Kerala Sports, a well planned system of physical training, attracting millions of youths to sports which will be developed through competent coaching and theoretical study will be the objective.

The why and what of a Master Plan

We are mindful that the ambitious title of this report is hardly justified by its contents, but it does emphasise four factors, (*a*) the abundance of human resources which can be turned to good 'athletic' account, (*b*) the present state of affairs in sports, (*c*) the possibilities of speedy development of the capabilities of our youth in Sports and Games, and (*d*) the vast outlay of trained men and money needed for elective use. We are comforted in the thought that this report will at least turn the spotlight on the petty done, the undone vast' in the athletic field and stimulate interest in the Sports Explosion potential of Kerala.

The Kerala Picture

A sense of dimension dawns on our minds when we realise that five young millions are students in Kerala today. At present, quasi-politics are the principal extracurricular occupation we permit our students, for, the existing sports facilities for the school going population are grossly inadequate and the inducement to them to play is still less. While the Kerala Education Rules and the relevant laws of the Universities of the State lay down an obligation on the managements to equip schools and colleges with playgrounds, these provisions are seldom enforced. On a random questioning, we discovered that hardly more than 5% of the students engage themselves in any games or athletics in the afternoons. Play grounds are scarce, equipment is poor or non-existent, coaches are few and the stimulus to turn out in the play fields or gymnasia to participate in public games and exercises little. So much so, working in a vicious circle, sport in the larger sense has become a Cinderella subject in the scholastic life of the student.

If the Kerala Education Rules are properly implemented and if the Government itself adopts the same guidelines for its own schools, there will be playgrounds for each institution. The colleges before they can get due legal recognition and affiliation to the University also must have enough space for playgrounds. Moreover, there are election in schools and colleges unions and sports receive attention at least formally. Games fees are collected although the way they are used either by Government or by private institutions leaves much to be desired.

We think it desirable to make provision for compulsory games and sports in the high school classes and above. Agreeing with report of the committee on Physical Education (U.G.C.) we think it essential to evolve an integrated scheme of physical education comprising games, sports, exercises, N.C.C. and allied activities which help develop physical fitness. One item must be obligatory, but which it should be will be left to the option of the student. Self-government even in games must being at the grass roots. An academic institution, for extra-curricular matters, must be transformed into a parliamentary microcesm with accountability, budgetary exercises in revenue and expenditure, planning, programming etc. in all departments of activity connected with their almamater. The idea is to guide students in physical education, make games and exercises obligatory and organise the functioning of the department with rights and answerability for performance being vested in the students themselves. I would therefore emphasise that from the lowest standard to the highest in our schools and from the lowest classes to the highest classes in colleges and Universities we must have both vertical and horizontal self-governing organisation, orientation and method.

The State must undertake the bulk of the capital investment in providing play grounds and buildings. As for consumable items and equipment, there must be substantial assistance by the Sports Councils at the State and District levels. The students themselves must contribute in the form of games fees. The entire amount must be utilised for the benefit of games and sports although as a fact what takes place now is to divert or accumulate or waste, thus producing dissatisfaction and a lack of responsibility among students.

Programmes for Student Youth

The Central Government and the various committees which have had occasion in the past to study the question of sports in India, have adopted a broad dichotomy for specialised attention. The student youth, starting from child to the senior college student, and the non-student youth embracing workers, white collared personnel, the armed services and the like, form two categories which should receive separate treatment. We propose to adopt a similar classification, not merely to fall into a set pattern but also because it is quite pragmatic.

The Kothari Commission on Education and National Development has glanced at the student fact of physical education which "contributes not only to physical fitness but also to physical efficiency, mental alertness and the development of certain qualities like perseverance, team spirit, leadership, obedience to rules, moderation in victory and balance in defeat". We may quote from the report the salient points of a satisfactory programme:

"(1) The physical education programme should be planned for desirable outcomes keeping in mind the interests and capacity of the participants.

(2) The traditional forms of play and physical activities that have developed in our country should receive due emphasis in the programme.

(3) The activities promoted should develop in each child a sense of personal worth and pride.

(4) A sense of sharing responsibility in a spirit of democratic co-operation should grow from experience on playground and also in the gymnasium.

(5) The programme offered should supplement other programmes of education and not duplicate them.

(6) The programme should be within financial means.

(7) The programme should reach all rather than a selected few.

(8) Special instruction and coaching should be provided for students with talent and special aptitude".

More or less on the same lines runs the Report of the Committee on Physical Education appointed by the University Grants Commission in December, 1965. "Though the aims and objectives of physical education have changed in emphasis with the needs and interests of people, physical fitness has always played an important part in the training of youth. In the context of the present situation, what is more important is that the value of physical education to total education and human development is being increasingly realised. While a University is mainly concerned with the imparting of existing knowledge as well as the advancement of knowledge by enquiry and investigation, and the transmission of cultural heritage from one generation to another, its functions are not limited to these ends alone. The University has also to develop the personality of the student in every aspect viz., physical, mental and emotional, and in the present context, to enable him to make his contribution to individual and social well-being by developing a sound and integrated programme of physical education".

Again, the said Report emphasises other facts of physical education. The progress of a country depends as much on the promotion of democratic values and social qualities, and the creation through it of a healthy corporate life, as on the success of its programmes for raising the standards of physical fitness. Physical education has come to be regarded all over the world as an essential part of education at the secondary and University levels. Even in this country, where it has received inadequate attention, no State or educational authority denies the need for it. But in practice, sufficiently energetic steps are not taken to promote it. The funds provided for promoting physical education in the Universities and Colleges are inadequate, and even the funds that are available are not as a rule properly utilised. As a result, facilities are, by and large, noticeably more inadequate in physical education than in other areas. To make things worse, there is a lack of interest on the part of students, teachers and educational authorities. The result is that programmes of physical education, especially at the University stage, are not understood or emphasised properly and are sometimes looked upon as even interfering with academic activities. The Committee is of the view that the development of physical education in the Universities and Colleges should be given the highest possible priority and regarded as an essential and integral part of education and human development. Apart from other consideration there is reason to believe that the absence of suitable provision for physical education is one of the major contributory causes of student unrest in the country". It is thus obvious that thinking Indian feel strongly - and we share that feeling - that student unrest and protest can be combated, in some measure, in the play-fields and gymnasia and so an energetic and comprehensive programme of sports and games in needed, not as a routine schemes to be mechanically prescribed nor as an occasional excitement or periodic thrill or heroic opportunity for an elite but as a mass elixir embracing large areas of the student population.

The National Programme

The All India pattern of orientation, development, and assistance in the matter of sports has taken clear shape although changes are taking places for the better founded on the experience gained over the years. The National Sports Coaching Scheme introduced first as the Rajkumari Sports Coaching Scheme has since been revised by the Board of Governors of the National Institute of Sports, and other Committees of experts have also made valuable suggestions for toning up the training and coaching of promising athletes. It is appropriate briefly to extract the objects of the National Sports Coaching Schemes:

(a) To assist the States in establishing and running of Regional Sports Coaching Centres to spot talent and help nurture it.

(b) To assist the Federations/Associations/Sports Boards and undertake, if necessary, Coaching of the National other teams for International and other competitions.

(c) To assist the states in running Coaching Camps approved by the State Sports Councils.

(d) To assist the National Federations/Associations in rendering coaching services, running clinics and organising competitions.

It is heartening that the Central Government goes to the extent of assisting the States in establishing and running of Regional Sports Coaching Centres and in spotting talent. The N.I.S. has agreed to establish one coaching centre in each State. They also supply essential consumable equipment and subsidise the maintenance expenditure to the extent of meeting the salaries of the Groundmen, Malis and Watchmen. Of course, the idea is that there will be a sports complex, in each State Centre. Co-operative effort by the States sports council, the central Agency and the local advisory committee will certainly prove fruitful, the State Government itself being called upon to provide the location of the Centre.

The National Sports Coaching Scheme visualize the discharge of certain functions by Regional Sports Coaching Centres such as catering to the needs of talented sportsmen, running of Orientation Courses of teachers and others connected with sports and games, organisation of short term Refresher Courses for district-level coaches in the State and helping organise seminars and clinics in the various games and sports in the State. Central assistance extends also to running of coaching camps, organising competitions etc.

While on paper all these large promises appear important, in practice the scanty stream of Central assistance and service leaves much to be desired in the student and the non-student areas. Moreover, considering the vast population to be covered and enormous extent of our country with its diversities and economic imbalances, there is a strong case for a tremendous increase in the scale and shape of assistance by the Central Government for sports development in the country. Of course, governmental impact must not savour of political pigmentation of Sports institutions.

Non-Student Youth of Kerala

The adult humanity of Kerala, *i.e.,* non-students, also needs a massive programme of sport. Indeed, in the present state of things, there is little nexus between plantation and farm labour, and public games or athletic exercises. Even the factory workers, barring a fringe, are alien to sports activities. We have no doubt that there must be a radical and massive change and revolutionary efforts must be made to bring into the fields and gyms and kalaries the rural population engaged in monotonous, manual work in farms and plantations. Similarly, the bulk of the work class in the factories as well as the clerical and office staff in the commercial wings of companies and firms, drudging away their days, must be induced to play some game or other. May be that many untrained and little known sportsmen remain unaware of their potentialities. We cannot allow "Chill penury" and the illiteracy of the Administration to "repress their noblerange". Indeed, the angry and "denied" worker and Clerk are a liability while enthusiastic sports activities flocking into the factories and offices may well be a rewarding investment. We have been disappointed that in the private as well as in the public sector, in the commercial firms and government concerns, in the high range plantations and the extensive fields on the plains, with a few exceptions, little is being done to freshen up the spirit and the physique of the employee through sports and games. We must and, later in this report, we have highlighted the obligation of Enterprises in this behalf.

Traditionally, Kerala has great martial art and indigenous physical culture patterns to be proud of. The land of Payattu and Thacholi Othenan, of Indian circus and Keeleri Kunhikannan and the training ground of yogic and other exercises cannot afford to undertake the need for the rediscovery of the role our native systems can play in preparing and promoting the ability and toughness of the physique of our youth. Small surprise, there is a successful though unscientifically surviving system of orthopedics and sports medicine. We must modernise these ancient treasures. In so doing, we must also take advantage of the natural resources of Kerala not merely in the shape of traditions and intelligence but also in the bounty of Nature. Kalaripayattu is a unique system of physical training as already mentioned, which will not only produce but prepare athletes and make the player one up as against his counter-parts without 'payattu'. The average Keralite, has an edge over his confeeres in the country on account of the diffusion of education among the people. This gives him and her an advantage even in Athletics and sports and games.

Our Land of Waters

Speaking of natural resources one cannot miss to mention the unique facility of vast sheets of water almost everywhere in Kerala which if properly exploited will make Kerala a paradise of water sport of every sport. Countries, less blessed, in this regard have exploited this factor to yield vastly greater sports dividends.

It is true that even now water sports and festivals during the Onam season are delightful and spectacular shows in our state, but then, we do not have any standards, rules and regulations in our scientific tests in organising these festivals and competitions. We have to regulate boat races under various heads and conduct them according to standardised rules. We have to have not mere gala shows but thrilling races which will be accepted as a product of skill and sportsmanship. Of course, apart from rowing, there are numerous other types of aquatic exercises which can easily be promoted among children and the grown-ups. Swimming, diving, water polo, water skiping, boat racing, surf riding and a joyous variety of aquatic sports can transform the sports face of this land of waters - given imagination and control and some financial backing.

Incentives

Sports festivals, inter-territorial, inter-collegiate and inter-university tournaments, frequent matches and coaching camps, and special credit for good performance are important items in the educational system that we visualise. Sustained interest can be created by giving a large number of scholarships and cash prizes for distinction in sports. Other things being more or less equal, preference should be given in matters of admission to professional courses and employment in the private and public sectors to those students who make a marks in games and sports.

Specialised training for students with special aptitude for games is desirable and special coaches must be appointed to train them up. Pooling for the raw materials at this level must be worked out and regional coaching centres must be started to impart specialised coaching. Hostels for sportsmen of promise from among students must be started or subsidised by the State, at least one in each District, so that special coaching in this department may not prejudice the curricular studies.

The Hungarian Example

It may not be out of place to state that a much smaller state than Indian has been trying the experiment of sports schools from which we could copy, adapt and orientate a system of spotting and training younger talent. I am extracting from the bulletin of the Hungarian Government dated 28th October 1970 which is at once informative and instructive.

"Every fifth inhabitant in Hungary, about 2 million young people, belong to the sports replacement age-group. These 8,00,000 boys and girls between the age of 6 and 18 are doing sports regularly, their cream talents selected for tournament sports, are trained in sports schools.

68 sports schools are active all over the country, 40 thousand children are trained in their different sections. The leaders of these schools are mostly eminent sportsmen.

"One part of these 10 years old sports schools operating within sports clubs, another part, called municipal sports schools, has been established at the county seats and is training the young talents of the town and environs. Last but not least there are sports schools which specialise in one single branch. All three types are given methodological advice by the Central Sports School in Budapest.

"The training of the up-and-coming in the sports schools has been based since the beginning of this term on the general schools with specialised sports curricula. The essence of this system is the following: new curriculum have been prepared for the specialise schools where, contrary to the traditional form, three gymnastics lesson a week are held in the first and the second grades, four lessons in the third and fourth and five lessons from the fifth to the eighth grades. The pupils of these schools will, however, not be at a disadvantage in any other subject, since the number of classes will not be reduced, on the contrary, the extra sports lessons are to raise the general number of weekly classes. These specialised schools are to guarantee the continous training of young talents."

Other Matters

We must insist upon every school appointing qualified physical instructors, and for every college one with a post graduate diploma or degree in physical education. The status and emoluments of these instructor and directors must be upgraded.

In the next five years, 50 per cent of the total academic community must be playing in the fields or exercising in the gyms. The programme of sports development in the rural areas may, perhaps, be organised by a measure of decentralization being injected into the system. We may have Block and District Sports Councils, each co-ordinating the activities within its area horizontally and forming part of the whole framework from the village to the capital vertically.

The Kerala Sports Bill

The need for an independent, high powered organisation which will co-ordinate, superintend and control sport in the State has landed us on the idea of a statue which will cover all aspects and vest overall responsibility and necessary powers in sports affairs in an autonomous body. We keenly feel that it is proper, indeed necessary, that there should be a minister in charge of sport and there should be a Kerala Sports Act, thus marrying sports projects and Executive concern for them to the rule of law.

Indian Sport is stated to be bedevilled by politics, cliques, poket boroughs etc. Therefore, it is all the more proper that we devise the protective and regulatory apparatus of a statue even in the field of sport. A legal framework with sufficient elbow room for the play of discretion, governmental and other, is in keeping with broad parliamentary control. In drafting a legislation in this behalf we have stuck to the democratic principle of elections and autonomy, gamewise and otherwise. The Sports Council, however, is being made the mainspring of sport life in the State. Every organisation and area of youth is welded into the machine and the Government itself is given weighty representation in the structure so that the authority and ability of the Sports Council may be considerable and even comparable with Universities and other important statutory bodies. Indeed the Sports Council may have even the need to start or run physical education colleges and sports institutions. Properly implemented, the prestigious office of President will command influence and ignite action. Transformation from the existing executive set-up to the statutory scaffolding is made smooth by transitory provisions. The statute has teeth, as it were, and litigation in the regular courts is excluded by a closed circuit system of internal adjudication. Government has a voice, a big one at that, as a delegate of the legislature in making rules and the minister in charge of sports, as in England, is the Chairman of the Sports Council. We express the hope that this pioneering legislative venture will receive wise and warm support from our legislators and that enough funds will be made available to make the sports system of Kerala viable. We have thought of a fee which will be marginal and will fall lightly on the upper income bracket only. The earmarking of a couple of lotteries by the state pump in finance for sport will be a fitting gesture. We ask for public support for this new direction in the sports movement of Kerala, particularly from the student youth and labour, for both of whom effective representation is being given in the sports council.

Men in uniform and while collared youth have received little attention in the matter of sports. The public organisation have almost ignored such adventures as irrelevant. Of course, the Police force is perhaps, the only organisation where sports activities receive some emphasis. More remains to be done even there and there should be no single policeman or woman whatever his age, who does not take part in athletic activities or play some game. We go further to recommend, that as a condition for recruitment, proficiency in sports should be prescribed in the Police and like services. We have suggested the I.G. of Police be made a Vice-President of the Sports Council ex-officio and expect the Police force in the State to lead other Government servants in the matter of Physical fitness.

State Institute of Sports

The success of the whole scheme consists in the availability of a large number of highly trained coaches and proficient trainers. There is no doubt that the present arrangement by which qualifications can be acquired only by a pilgrimage to Patiala and a long sojourn there, can hardly be satisfactory. We must have a national institute of sports in the South. But Kerala cannot wait till the long incubation period for finalisation of such a proposal passes. Therefore, it is suggested by our Committee, that there be a State Institute of Sports in Trivandrum, upgrading the existing Physical Education College and reorganising it on the lines of the N.I.S. Patiala. Degrees and Diplomas must be conferred, new departments of knowledge, like sport medicine, must be started, research into indigenous art and other sports matters must be organised. On the whole, a new national dimension should be imparted to the Institution. Think it important that a Calicut or Tellicherry a Circus College is also started which may be integrated with sports development in the state. Indeed, circus in India was, perhaps, born and fostered in North Kerala and there is no reason why this exciting art should not inspire the starting of a Circus Training Institution. As an integral but important part thereof, a Kalari Payattu wing may also be opened in that College.

These are not fanciful ideas beyond the budgetary digestion of the State. What we need is the enlightened will to put Kerala on the Sports map of India in a big way. Money is secondary and when it comes to actual working out of the financial implications of our Report and their implementation by way of phased programmes, the Government may not be inhibited from giving effect to the schemes and projects by financial consideration. Less politics in sport and more sports in politics, we pray, will give a sporting chance for the proposals we have made in this Report of the hands and the heads at the Legislators who ultimately count in a democratic polity.

Index